A Life of Galileo

Bertolt Brecht was born in Augsburg on 10 February 1898 and died in Berlin on 14 August 1956. He grew to maturity as a playwright in the frenetic years of the twenties and early thirties, with such plays as *Man Equals Man*, *The Threepenny Opera* and *The Mother*. He left Germany when Hitler came to power in 1933, eventually reaching the United States in 1941, where he remained until 1947. It was during this period of exile that such masterpieces as *Life of Galileo*, *Mother Courage and Her Children* and *The Caucasian Chalk Circle* were written. Shortly after his return to Europe in 1947, he founded the Berliner Ensemble, and from then until his death was mainly occupied in producing his own plays.

Mark Ravenhill's previous work includes *Ten Plagues*; *Ghost Story*; *Nation*; *The Experiment*; *Over There*; *A Life in Three Acts* (co-written with Bette Bourne); *Shoot/Get Treasure/Repeat*; *Ripper*; *pool (no water)*; *Dick Whittington and His Cat*; *Citizenship*; *The Cut*; *Product*; *Education*; *Moscow*; *Totally Over You*; *Mother Clap's Molly House*; *North Greenwich*; *Some Explicit Polaroids*; *Handbag*; *Sleeping Around*; *Faust is Dead* and *Shopping and F***ing*.

Bertolt Brecht

A Life of Galileo

English translation by
Mark Ravenhill

from a literal translation by Deborah Gearing

Original work entitled
Leben des Galilei

Bloomsbury Methuen Drama
An imprint of Bloomsbury Publishing Plc

B L O O M S B U R Y

LONDON • NEW DELHI • NEW YORK • SYDNEY

Bloomsbury Methuen Drama
An imprint of Bloomsbury Publishing Plc

Imprint previously known as Methuen Drama

50 Bedford Square	1385 Broadway
London	New York
WC1B 3DP	NY 10018
UK	USA

www.bloomsbury.com

BLOOMSBURY, METHUEN DRAMA and the Diana logo are trademarks of Bloomsbury Publishing Plc

This translation by Mark Ravenhill first published 2013,
from a literal translation by Deborah Gearing
Reprinted 2013 (twice), 2014, 2015

Methuen Drama series editor for Bertolt Brecht: Tom Kuhn

Original work entitled *Leben des Galilei*
See Bertolt Brecht Stücke 5 (Groß commentierte Berliner
und Frankfurter Ausgabe) Aufbau and Suhrkamp 1988

British Library Cataloguing-in-Publication Data
A catalogue record for this book is available from the British Library.

ISBN: PB: 978-1-4725-0741-9
ePDF: 978-1-4725-1398-4
ePUB: 978-1-4725-0803-4

Library of Congress Cataloging-in-Publication Data
A catalogue record for this book is available from the British Library.

Series: Modern Plays

Typeset by Mark Heslington Ltd, Scarborough, North Yorkshire

A Life of Galileo

Characters

Galileo Galilei
Andrea Sarti
Mrs Sarti
Ludovico Marsili
Bursar
Sagredo
Virginia
Federonzi
The Doge
Senators
Cosimo de Medici
Chamberlain
Philosopher
Mathematician
The older court lady
The younger court lady
A fat prelate
Two scholars
Two monks
Two astronomers
A very thin monk
A very old cardinal
Father Christopher Clavius
The little monk
The Cardinal Inquisitor
Cardinal Barberini, later Pope
Cardinal Bellarmin
Two ecclesiastical secretaries
Two young ladies
Gaffone, Rector
Ballad Singer
His wife
Vanni
An official
A person
A monk
A peasant
Guard
Clerk
Boy
Girl

One

Galileo Galilei, *teacher of mathematics in Padua, wants to prove the Copernican system.*

In the year sixteen hundred and nine
The light of science shone
In a modest house in Padua
As Galileo set out to prove
That the sun is fixed
And the earth is on the move

Galileo*'s shabby study in Padua. Morning.* **Andrea**, *the housekeeper's son, brings a glass of a milk and a bread roll.*

Galileo (*washing his upper body, puffing with pleasure*.)   Milk on the table. Don't shut any of my books.

Andrea   Ma says: we've got to pay the milkman and if we don't, he's going to be running rings around the house, Galileo.

Galileo   Describing a circle, Andrea.

Andrea   Alright then. If we don't pay the milkman, he will be describing a circle around us.

Galileo   Whereas the bailiff comes at us in a straight line by finding the –

Andrea   shortest

Galileo   – journey between

Andrea   two points.

Galileo   Excellent.

Andrea *spots a model of the Ptolemaic system.*

Andrea   What's that?

Galileo   That shows how the stars push themselves around the Earth according to dead philosophers.

Andrea   How?

Galileo   Let's make a study. Begin at the beginning: description.

Andrea   In the middle there's a pebble.

Galileo   The Earth.

Andrea   All around it, one on top of the other – rings.

Galileo   Numbering?

Andrea   Eight.

Galileo   The crystal spheres.

Andrea   On the rings there are balls.

Galileo   The stars.

Andrea   They've got little flags on them. Painted words.

Galileo   What words?

Andrea   Names of stars.

Galileo   For example?

Andrea   The ball at the bottom says moon. The one on top says sun.

Galileo   Now let the sun spin.

Andrea (*moves the spheres*)   It's beautiful. But the Earth is so trapped.

Galileo (*drying himself*)   Just how I felt the first time I was shown it. Some of us feel like that. (*Throws* **Andrea** *a towel so he can dry his back.*) No room.

For two thousand years men have believed that the sun and all the stars in heaven spin around them.

The Pope, cardinals, princes, scholars, captains, merchants, women selling fish, school children: all believed they were sitting there motionless in the middle of that crystal ball.

We're heading off, Andrea, headlong into space. The old age has passed, this is a new age. For the past hundred years, it's as though humanity has been anticipating something.

Our cities are cramped, so are our minds. Superstition, plague. But now we say: that's the way it is, doesn't mean that's the way it has to stay. Everything's moving.

I like to think it began with the ships. Ever since man can remember all they did was creep along the coasts but then suddenly they left the coasts and sped out across the seas.

A rumour started: there are new continents. So we sent ships to the 'New World'. And now the continents laugh and say: the sea which we feared so much is a puddle.

A huge hunger has risen to explore the cause of everything: why a stone falls when we drop it and why it goes up when we chuck it up in the air. Every day we discover something new. Old people get young people to shout in their ears: what's the latest discovery.

We've found out so much but there's so much more to find. And so there's always new things for new generations to discover.

Where faith sat for thousands of years, there now stands doubt. All the world says: yes we know what's written in the books but now let's see what our eyes tell us.

And so a breeze is blowing and it lifts up the gold-hemmed skirts of princes and prelates and underneath are legs – fat and thin legs – just like our legs. Heaven – it turns out – is empty. And we let out a great happy laugh.

I predict, in our lifetimes, they'll be talking about astronomy in the market square. The fishwife's son will race to school. Knowledge-hungry people will dance in the streets when they see that a new astronomy has put the Earth on the move.

And as the Earth rolls happily around the sun so the sellers of fish and merchants and princes and cardinals and yes even the Pope roll with it too.

Overnight, the cosmos has lost its centre. But come the morning, there will be many, many, countless centres. Because now we're all at the centre. Or none of us are. But there is so much more room.

Andrea   Drink your milk. You've got people want to see you.

Galileo   Before that, did you grasp what I told you yesterday?

Andrea   What? Kippernikus and the turning stuff?

Galileo   Yes.

Andrea   No. Why do you want me to understand it? It's really difficult.

Galileo   It's important that you understand it. That's why I work and buy books instead of paying the milkman – so that people like you can understand it.

Andrea   But I look and I see: the sun in the evening isn't in the same place as it was in the morning. So it can't be standing still, can it?

Galileo   You see. What? You see nothing. You just gawp. Gawping isn't seeing.

He puts the wash stand in the middle of the room.

That's the sun. Sit.

Andrea *sits in a chair.* **Galileo** *stands behind him.*

Where's the sun – right or left?

Andrea   Left.

Galileo   And how does it get to the right?

Andrea   You carry it to the right. Obviously.

Galileo   The only way?

Picks him up in the chair, makes a half turn.

Where's the sun?

Andrea   On the right.

Galileo   Has it moved?

Andrea   No.

Galileo   So what's moved?

Andrea   Me.

Galileo (*shouts*)   Wrong! Moron! The chair!

Andrea   With me on it!

Galileo   Obviously. The chair is the Earth. And you're sitting on it.

Mrs Sarti (*who has been watching*)   There's a young man downstairs looking for private tuition. Smart clothes. Letter of recommendation. (*Gives* **Galileo** *the letter.*) What are you doing to my boy Galileo? Why do you tell him all this rubbish? He chats about it in school and then the priest comes to me and warns me that he's spoken unholy words. You should be ashamed Galileo.

Galileo   Andrea and I have made discoveries that we can no longer keep secret from the world. A new age, a great age is beginning in which it is bliss to be alive.

Mrs Sarti   Well, let's hope in the new age we can pay the milkman. (*Pointing to letter of recommendation.*) Do us a favour. Don't send this one away. Milk bill.

Exit.

Galileo (*laughing*)   I like milk.

Andrea   But it's not true. You only moved the chair sideways. Not like this. (*Makes arm movement forwards.*) Otherwise I would have actually fallen off the chair. Why didn't you turn the chair upside down? Because it would have proved that I'd fall off the Earth. Got you.

Galileo (*takes apple*)   Right. This is the Earth.

Andrea   With examples you can prove anything if you're cunning, Galileo.

Galileo (*puts apple back*)   Alright then. If you want to remain a moron.

Andrea   Pick it up again. So why don't I end up upside down at night?

Galileo   So this is the Earth and here you are standing on it. (*Sticks a splinter of wood in the apple.*) And now the Earth turns.

Andrea   And I'm hanging upside down.

Galileo   Really? Look at it properly. Where's your head?

Andrea   There. Underneath.

Galileo   Is it? (*Turns it back.*) Isn't it exactly where it was? Are your feet still on the Earth? Or did I do this? (*Takes out the splinter and turns it around.*)

Andrea   So why can't I see that I'm turning?

Galileo   Because you're turning with the Earth.

Andrea   And why does it look as though the sun is moving?

Galileo (*turning apple with the splinter again*)   Underneath you is the Earth. It stays the same, always underneath you. But now the lamp's above your head but now I turn it and what's above your head?

Andrea   The bowl.

Galileo   And where's the lamp?

Andrea   Underneath.

Galileo   Aha!

Enter **Ludovico**, *a rich young man.*

Galileo   One more pigeon come to the loft.

Ludovico   Good morning, sir. Ludovico Marsili.

Galileo (*studying the letter*)   You've been in Holland. Your family own land near Rome.

Ludovico   Mother wanted me to take a look around, see what's going on in the world.

Galileo   And in Holland they told you that in Italy I'm what's going on ?

Ludovico   Mother says I should know some science.

Galileo   Private lessons: ten scudi a month.

Ludovico   Certainly.

Galileo   What interests you?

Ludovico   Horses.

Galileo   Uh.

Ludovico   I'm not very suited to science.

Galileo   Then let's call it fifteen scudi a month.

Ludovico   Right you are.

Galileo   I'll have to see you first thing in the morning. Which means I won't be teaching you, Andrea.

Andrea   Can I have the apple?

Galileo   Yes.

Andrea *exits.*

Ludovico   Be patient with me. Science always seems to be at odds with common sense. Like this funny tube that they're selling in Amsterdam. I've had a close look. A sleeve of green leather and two lenses one like this (*Indicates concave.*) and one like this (*Convex.*). I'm told one lens makes things bigger, the other makes things smaller. A sensible person would say: they cancel each other out. Not so. Look through the thing and everything far away – spires, pigeons – five times bigger. Science.

Galileo   You yourself have seen spires magnified?

Ludovico   I have.

Galileo   Two lenses? (*Makes a sketch.*) Like this? (**Ludovico** *nods.*) How old is this invention?

Ludovico   I believe when I left Holland it had been on the market for a couple of days.

Galileo   Are you sure you need science? What about horse gelding?

Mrs Sarti *enters unseen by* **Galileo**.

Ludovico   Mother says it has to be science.

Galileo   Choose a dead language or theology. Much easier. (*Sees* **Sarti**.) Terrific. See you Tuesday morning.

Ludovico *exits*.

Galileo   Don't give me that look. I've taken him.

Sarti   Because you saw me just in time. The bursar from the university's outside.

Galileo   Show him in. He's important. Could be worth 500 scudi. Then I won't need any pupils.

Sarti *shows in the* **Bursar**. **Galileo** *has finished dressing, while he scribbles on a piece of paper.*

Galileo   Morning. Lend us half a scudo.

The **Bursar** *gets the coin out of a purse and* **Galileo** *passes it on to* **Sarti**.

Sarti, send Andrea out for a couple of lenses. Measurements.

Sarti *leaves with the paper.*

Bursar   I come regarding your request for an increase of your salary to 1,000 scudi. I'm sorry to say that I can't recommend this. As you know, departments of mathematics don't bring in great numbers to the university.

Galileo   I can't manage on 500 scudi.

Bursar   Galileo, you lecture twice a week for two hours. With your extraordinary reputation surely you must attract huge numbers of students willing to pay for private lessons?

Galileo   Too many of them. I teach and I teach and when am I supposed to learn? I'm not as stuffed with knowledge as the gentlemen of the philosophy faculty. I'm stupid. I understand nothing. I need to fill up all these gaps in my knowledge. And when am I going to do that? When will I research? My science is hungry to learn. We're presented with new problems and all we have are hypotheses. We must challenge ourselves to find proof.

Bursar   May I remind you that although our Republic does not pay as much as certain principalities, we do guarantee freedom of research. Everyone knows that in our Republic the Inquisition has no sway. That must be worth something to you, an astronomer working in a field which the church has for so long now regarded with less than respect.

Galileo   Good for your balance sheet isn't it? Elsewhere the Inquisition is sticking people on the fire and you get excellent cut-price academics.

Bursar   Unfair! Unfair!

Galileo   What good is freedom of research without the free time to do the researching? Perhaps you could show your colleagues my researches into the laws of falling bodies (*A pile of papers.*) and ask them if that's not worth a couple of scudi.

Bursar   What's worth scudi is what brings in scudi. Your laws of falling bodies have certainly been a sensation. They're singing your praises in Paris and Prague. But all that praise doesn't bring our university any income.

Galileo   I get it. Freedom to research as long as it brings free trade, yes?

Bursar   Galileo! I don't understand your cynicism. The flourishing trade balance of our republic is not a thing to despise. Nobody here will allow your work to be disturbed, the authorities don't make things difficult for you. Admit it Galileo – here, you can work.

Galileo (*in despair*)   Yes.

Bursar   Make something nice again. Like your excellent proportional compasses.

Galileo   Child's play.

Bursar   Which delighted and amazed the nobility and brought in money.

Galileo   You've given me an idea. Maybe I've got something for you.

He picks up the sheet with the sketch.

Bursar   Yes? That could solve our problem. Galileo, we know you're a great man. A great but – if I might say so – a dissatisfied man.

Galileo   Yes I am dissatisfied and you'd pay me for that if you had any sense. Because I'm dissatisfied with myself. I'm more than halfway through my life and I'm not satisfied with anything that I've achieved.

Bursar   Then I won't disturb you any longer.

Galileo   Thank you.

*The **Bursar** exits.*

Galileo *remains alone for a while and then begins work.* **Andrea** *runs in.*

Galileo   You didn't eat your apple.

Andrea   I'm going to use it to show how the Earth turns.

Galileo   Andrea, listen to me. Don't talk to other people about our ideas.

Andrea   Why not?

Galileo   We scientists can't prove that what we believe is fact. Even the teachings of the great Copernicus aren't proven. Just a hypothesis. Give me the lenses.

Andrea   Half a scudo wasn't enough. I had to give them my coat.

Galileo   What will you do without a coat in winter?

Galileo *arranges the lenses on the paper using the sketch.*

Andrea   What's a hypothesis?

Galileo   It's when you think that something is probable but you don't have the facts. Pretty woman down there in front of the basket makers' shop, holding her child to her breast, she's giving milk to the baby not receiving milk from it. That's a hypothesis until you go down there and see it and prove it. We look up at the stars but we're like worms with dull eyes who can barely see. The old teachings are in ruins, so many old laws which explain so little while our new hypotheses have so few laws but explain so much.

Andrea   Galileo, I want to be a physicist too.

Galileo   Very wise – it's a field in which there are so many questions to be answered.

He has moved to the window and has looked through the lenses. Moderately interested.

Take a look Andrea.

Andrea   Mother of God, everything's so close. The bell on the Campanile – really close. I can even read the copper letters: Gracia dei.

Galileo   Should be worth 500 scudi.

Two

Galileo *presents the Republic of Venice with his new discovery.*

Not everything a great man does is good
And Galileo enjoyed his food
So listen without anger as we show
The truth about the telescope

The Great Arsenal of Venice at the harbour. **Senators**, *at their head,
the* **Doge**. *To one side* **Galileo**'s *friend* **Sagredo** *and the fifteen-
year-old* **Virginia Galilei** *with a velvet cushion, on which rests a
telescope, about 60cm long with a bright red leather casing.* **Galileo**
on a dais. Behind him is the stand for the telescope, looked after by
Federonzi *the lens grinder.*

Galileo   Your Excellency. As teacher of mathematics at your
university in Padua and director of your Great Arsenal here
in Venice, I have always prided myself that not only do I
fulfil my exalted teaching commission but also that I bring
great advantages to our Republic with practical inventions.
With great joy and deep humility I will today present and
demonstrate a completely new instrument, the spyglass,
researched by your loyal servant for seventeen years.

Galileo (*quietly to* **Sagredo**)   I'm wasting time.

Sagredo   You'll be able to pay the milk bill.

Bursar (*steps on to the dais*)   Excellency. Once more the great
book of learning is inscribed with the Venetian hand. (*Polite
applause.*) A great scholar of world renown presents to you,
and only you, this tube, ready to manufacture and launch on
the market, as you see fit. (*Louder applause.*) With this
instrument will be able to see enemy ships a full two hours
before they see us. (*Very loud applause.*) And now Your
Excellency please accept this marvel of invention, witness of
Galileo's wisdom, from the hand of his charming daughter.
(*Applause.*)

Music. **Virginia** *steps forward, bows, presents the telescope to the*
Bursar, *who gives it to* **Federonzi**. **Federonzi** *puts it on the stand*

and adjusts it. The **Doge** *and the* **Senators** *step on to the dais and look through the tube.*

Galileo (*quietly*)   I'm not sure I can sit through this performance. They look and they see a money-making toy. But it's so much more than that. Last night, I pointed that tube at the moon.

Sagredo   What did you see?

Galileo   The moon doesn't emit its own light.

Sagredo   What?

Senator   There's the fortifications of Santa Rosita – They're eating fish on that boat. Fried fish. Making me hungry.

Galileo   Astronomy has been stuck for a thousand years because it needed a telescope.

Senator   With that thing you can see too much. From now on, I shall forbid my women to bathe on the roof.

Galileo   Do you know what makes up the Milky Way?

Sagredo   No.

Galileo   I do.

Senator   Galileo, we could market this at ten scudi per tube.

Galileo *bows.*

Virginia (*brings* **Ludovico** *to her father*)   Father, Father, Ludovico wants to congratulate you Father.

Ludovico (*embarrassed*)   Congratulations.

Galileo   I've improved it.

Ludovico   Yes sir. You've made the casing red.

Galileo (*to* **Sagredo**)   I think I might be able to prove a certain hypothesis with that thing.

Sagredo   One step at a time.

Bursar   Galileo, your 500 scudi are in the bag.

Galileo (*ignoring him*)   I won't of course rush to any conclusions.

The **Bursar** *leads* **Galileo** *to the* **Doge** *and the* **Senators** *who encircle him.* **Virginia** *and* **Ludovico** *walk away slowly.*

Virginia   Did I do something wrong?

Ludovico   Not at all.

Virginia   But you're annoyed?

Ludovico   Oh nothing.

Virginia   I think everyone is very pleased with Father.

Ludovico   And I think I'm beginning to understand a thing or two about science.

Three

10 January 1610. Using the telescope, **Galileo** *proves the Copernican system. Warned by his friend of the possible consequences of his discoveries,* **Galileo** *proclaims his belief in human reason.*

The tenth of January, sixteen ten:
Galileo saw there was no heaven

Galileo's *study in Padua. Night.* **Galileo** *and* **Sagredo**, *wrapped in thick coats, at the telescope.*

Sagredo (*looking through the telescope, quietly*)   The edge of the moon is irregular, indentations, rough. On the dark side, close to the light side, there are light points. From these points, the light increases over further areas until it comes together with the light part.

Galileo   How do you explain the light parts?

Sagredo   It's not possible.

Galileo   Yes it is. They're mountains.

Sagredo   On a star?

Galileo   Huge mountains. The sun illuminates those light points while it's still night on the slopes. As you watch the light comes down from the high peaks and into the valleys.

Sagredo   But that contradicts two thousand years of astronomy.

Galileo   Yes it does. You're looking at something that no man has seen apart from me. You're the second.

Sagredo   But the moon is a star. It can't have mountains and valleys.

Galileo   An ordinary heavenly body, one amongst thousands. Look again. The dark side of the moon: is it completely dark?

Sagredo   No. There's a faint ash-coloured light.

Galileo   Which comes from the Earth.

Sagredo   Impossible. How can the Earth give off light, with its mountains and forests and seas, a cold body?

Galileo   Same way as the moon gives off light. Because we're both lit up by the sun. If you looked at us from the moon, you'd see us sometimes as a crescent, sometimes full, sometimes not at all.

Sagredo   You're telling me there's no difference between the moon and the Earth?

Galileo   So it seems.

Sagredo   Ten years ago in Rome they burned Giordano Bruno for saying that.

Galileo   They did. But still it's there. Keep looking, Sagredo. Today, the tenth of January 1610, humanity notes in its diary: heaven gone.

Sagredo   That's terrible.

Galileo   I've discovered something else. Possibly even more important.

Sarti (*entering*)   The Bursar.

Bursar *rushes in.*

Bursar   Forgive the late hour. I would speak with you alone.

Galileo   Sagredo can hear anything that I hear.

Bursar   It may not be pleasant for you if the gentleman hears this. It is something quite incredible.

Galileo   Sagredo is used to hearing the incredible when he's with me.

Bursar   I'm sure he is. (*Pointing to the telescope.*) That thing: completely worthless.

Sagredo (*who has been walking around restlessly*)   Why?

Bursar   Did you know that your invention is on sale on every street corner for a couple of scudi? And that it's made in Holland? Even now there's a Dutch freighter in the harbour unloading 500 telescopes.

Galileo   Really?

Sagredo   Mr Pruili, I can't judge the worth of this instrument for trade but its worth for philosophy is so immeasurable that –

Bursar   Philosophy. What has Galileo, a mathematician, got to do with philosophy? Galileo, you once invented for the city a water pump and some very useful irrigation works. And now – this.

Galileo   Sea routes are still unmapped, costly. We need a clock in the sky, a navigator's signpost. With the telescope we can see the stars clearly, follow their regular movements. New astronomical charts could save shipping millions of scudi.

Bursar   Forget it. I've already heard enough. I gave you a helping hand and you've made me a joke across the city. I say this to you and I say it as an honest man: I am disgusted by this world!

He exits, slamming the door behind him.

Galileo   I like him when he's angry. 'Disgusting. A world in which you can't do business'.

Sagredo   Did you know about the Dutch telescope?

Galileo   How can I work with the bailiff in the room? And soon Virginia will need a dowry, she's not bright. And I like to buy books. And good food. Miserable age! If I'd had five years of free time for research I could have proved everything! I'm showing you something else.

Sagredo (*hesitating to go to the telescope*)   I'm feeling something very close to fear.

Galileo   I'm showing you one of the shining fogs of the Milky Way. Tell me what it consists of.

Sagredo   Stars. Too many to count.

Galileo   In the constellation of Orion alone there are 500 stars, many worlds, countless others.

Sagredo   That's still a long way from Copernicus' theory that the Earth turns round the sun. There's no star in the sky that has another turning around it, as the moon turns round the Earth.

Galileo   I wonder. For the last couple of days, I've wondered. Jupiter. (*Adjusts the telescope.*) Through the tube, you can see four smaller stars near to it. I saw them on Monday but didn't take any special notice of their position. I looked again yesterday. I could have sworn all four had changed position. I noted them. They're different again today. What? I saw four. (*Agitated.*) Take a look!

Sagredo   I can see three.

Galileo   Where's the fourth one? Charts. We must chart their movements.

They set to work excitedly. It becomes dark on stage but on the cyclorama we can still see Jupiter and its moons. When it's light again, they are still sitting there, winter coats on.

Galileo   Proof. The fourth star must have gone behind Jupiter so we can't see it. Jupiter is a star around which another one turns.

Sagredo   And the crystal sphere to which Jupiter is attached?

Galileo   How can Jupiter be attached to a crystal sphere if other stars circle around it? There's no prop in the heavens, there's no support in space!

Sagredo   You're thinking too quickly.

Galileo   Too quickly. You're seeing what no one has ever seen. He was right.

Sagredo   Copernicus?

Galileo   The whole world was against him and he was right. I've got to show Andrea.

Excited, he runs to the door and shouts.

Sarti! Sarti!

Sagredo   Galileo, you must calm down.

Galileo   You should get excited. Sarti!

Sagredo (*turning the telescope away*)   Stop bellowing like a fool.

Galileo   You stop standing there like a herring in brine when the truth is discovered.

Sagredo   I'm terrified because it could be true.

Galileo   What?

Sagredo   Have you lost your mind? Don't you understand what's going to happen if what you see here is true? If you shout it out in the market square: the Earth is just a star and not the centre of the universe. That there is nothing but stars. And where is God?

Galileo   What do you mean?

Sagredo   Where's God?

Galileo   I'm a scientist.

Sagredo   But above all else, you're a human being. And I ask you in your cosmology where is God?

Galileo   In all of us or nowhere.

Sagredo   That's why he was burned. Less than ten years ago.

Galileo   Because he had no proof. Only a hypothesis. Sarti! Sagredo, I believe in humanity which means I believe in reason. If I didn't believe in that I wouldn't be strong enough to get out of bed in the morning.

Sagredo   Then I'll tell you something: I don't believe in humanity. Forty or so years amongst people and I've learnt this: they're not open to reason. Show them a fiery comet's tail, something to drive a little fright into them, and they will tear out of their houses and fall and break their legs. But say one sensible sentence to them and then prove it with seven arguments and they'll mock you.

Galileo   That is a lie and a slander. How can you believe that, you who love science. The only thing that can't be reasoned with is a corpse.

Sagredo   How can you mistake mankind's pitiful cunning for reason!

Galileo   I'm not talking about their cunning. I know they call a donkey a horse when they're selling and a horse a donkey when they're buying. That's cunning. But the old woman who with her rough hands puts out an extra bale of hay for the mule on the evening before the journey, the sailor who checks for storms before he shops for supplies, the child who wears a hat when she's been given evidence that it might rain, these are my hope because they're using reason. Yes I believe in the gentle power of human reason. No one can go on watching me drop a stone (*Lets a stone fall from his pocket to the floor.*) and say: it doesn't fall. No human can do that. In time, they can't resist it. Proof seduces them. One of the greatest pleasures of the human race is thinking.

Sarti (*enters*)   Do you need something Galileo?

Galileo (*who is back at his telescope, making notes, very friendly*)   Andrea.

Sarti   Asleep.

Galileo   Can't you wake him?

Sarti   What do you need him for?

Galileo   To show him something which no person apart from us has seen since the Earth began.

Sarti   Through your tube?

Galileo   Through my tube.

Sarti   He needs his sleep.

Galileo   Perhaps then Sarti you can help me. A question has come up on which we can't agree probably because we've read too many books. It's a question about the stars. It goes like this: does the big thing turn around the small or the small around the big?

Sarti (*suspiciously*)   Is this a serious question or are you laughing at me again?

Galileo   Serious question.

Sarti   Then I'll give you a quick answer. Do I serve you food or do you serve me?

Galileo   You serve me. Yesterday it was burnt.

Sarti   Because in the middle of the cooking, little me had to bring you your big boots.

Galileo   So you did.

Sarti   Head in a book but he pays.

Sarti, *amused, goes.*

Galileo   And people like that don't want the truth? They grab it with both hands.

A bell for early mass has begun to ring. **Virginia** *enters in a coat, carrying a lantern.*

Virginia   Good morning Father.

Galileo   Why are you up so early?

Virginia   I'm going to early mass with Mrs Sarti. Ludovico's joining us. How was the night?

Galileo   Bright.

Virginia   Can I have a look?

Galileo   Why?

Virginia *doesn't know how to reply.*

It's not a toy.

Virginia   Have you seen something new in the heavens?

Galileo   Nothing for you. Virginia we may be moving to Florence. I've written a letter to the Grand Duke there asking if he needs me as court mathematician.

Virginia (*smiling*)   At court?

Sagredo   Galileo.

Galileo   I need free time. I need to find proof. And I want some earthly delights. I can't stand up in front of the whole world without proof. And there's still not a single proof that any heavenly body circles around the sun. And I must prove that, prove that to everyone from Sarti to the Pope. My only worry is that the court won't have me.

Virginia   Of course they'll have you Father with the new stars and everything.

Galileo   Go to mass.

Virginia *goes.*

Galileo   Not often that I write to important people.

He gives letter to **Sagredo**.

Don't you think I've done it rather well?

Sagredo (*reads aloud the end of the letter*)   'For I long for nothing so much as I long to be closer to you the rising sun which shines so brightly upon our age'. Galileo. The Grand Duke of Florence is nine years old.

Galileo   You think it's too grovelling? I wonder if I've grovelled enough, whether I'd prostrated myself sufficiently to show true devotion. I despise a person whose brain is incapable of filling his belly.

Sarti *and* **Virginia** *pass by the men to go to mass.*

Sagredo   Don't go to Florence Galileo.

Galileo   Why not?

Sagredo   Because the monks have power there.

Galileo   At the court there are great scholars.

Sagredo   Yes-men.

Galileo   I'll grab them by the head and drag them to the tube. The monks are people too. They'll be seduced by proof. Copernicus asked that they believe a hypothesis. All I ask is that they believe their eyes.

Sagredo   Galileo, you've chosen a dark path. When a person sees the truth it's a night of disaster. And an hour of delusion when he believes in the reason of the human race. Who walks seeing all before him? The man who walks to the scaffold. How can the powerful let a man walk free when he knows the truth, right to the furthest stars. Do you think the Pope will listen to the truth? Do you think he'll write in his diary '10 January 1610: heaven gone'? How can you leave the Republic carrying the truth in your pocket, the tube in your hand, into the traps of princes and monks? So careful in your science, so credulous with everything that seems to ease its pursuit. Just now when you were looking at the new stars I thought I saw you standing in the flames and as you spoke of proof I smelled flesh burning. I love science but more than that I love you. Don't go to Florence Galileo.

Galileo   If they'll have me, I'll go.

Four

Galileo *has exchanged the Republic of Venice for the Court of Florence. His discoveries are not believed by the court scholars.*

The old says: I'm like this because that's how I've always
    been.
The new says: If you're no use, then it's time to go.

Galileo*'s house in Florence. The* **Grand Duke of Tuscany**, **Cosimo de Medici**, *the court* **Chamberlain**, *two women courtiers*, **Galileo**, **Federonzi**, *professors from the university*, **Sarti**, **Andrea**.

Galileo (*at the telescope*)   As I'm sure Your Highness knows, for some time now we astronomers have been having some problems with our calculations. We use a very old system, which is consistent with philosophy but alas doesn't fit the facts. According to the old system, the movements of the stars are extremely complicated. For example, the planet Venus is said to execute a movement like this.

He draws the epicyclic course of Venus according to the Ptolemaic system.

But even with a movement like this, we still can't predict the position of the stars correctly. They turn up in places where they're not supposed to be. In addition, there are movements of the stars which this old system can't explain. Recently I have discovered exactly such movements around the planet Jupiter. Would the gentlemen agree to begin our viewing with the satellites of Jupiter, the Medici stars?

Andrea (*pointing to a stool at the telescope*)   Please take a seat here.

Philosopher   Thank you. I'm afraid it's not quite so simple. Galileo before we make use of your famous tube, we would like to request the pleasure of a debate. Subject: can such planets exist?

Galileo   I thought you'd just look through the telescope and see for yourselves?

Andrea   Here, please.

Mathematician   Yes, yes – You do know of course that according to the ancients a star which turns around a point other than the Earth and stars which have no support in the sky are not possible?

Galileo   Yes.

Philosopher   And quite apart from the possibility of such stars, which the mathematician (*He bows to the* **Mathematician**.) appears to doubt, may I, as a humble philosopher, pose the question: are such stars necessary? *Aristoteles divini ursum* –

Galileo   Can we talk in plain language? My colleague, Federonzi, doesn't understand Latin.

Philosopher   Is it important that he understands us?

Galileo   Yes.

Philosopher   I'm sorry. I thought he was your lens grinder.

Andrea   A lens grinder and a scholar.

Philosopher   If Federonzi insists.

Galileo   I insist.

Philosopher   The argument will lose brilliance but it's your house. The universe of the great Aristotle, its celestial musical spheres, crystalline vaults, the turning of its heavenly bodies, the inspired construction of the sphere of heaven, is a system of such order and beauty that we should hesitate to disturb its harmony.

Galileo   Your Highness why don't you come and look at these impossible and unnecessary stars through the telescope?

Mathematician   One is tempted to reply that your tube, in showing us what cannot be, must not – must it not? – be a very reliable tube?

Galileo   What do you mean?

Mathematician   It would be so much more expeditious, Galileo, if you told us the reasons which move you to the supposition that in the furthest sphere of the immutable heavens there are other stars which support themselves and jiggle about.

Philosopher   Reasons, Galileo, reasons.

Galileo   Reasons? When you can look at the stars themselves?

Cosimo (*looks round to the ladies of the court*)   Is something not right with my stars?

Older Lady (*to* **Grand Duke**)   Everything is fine with Your Highness' stars. The gentlemen are just wondering if they're really there.

Pause.

Younger Lady   I've heard you can see every wheel on the Plough through that tube.

Federonzi   Yes and plenty more on the Bull.

Galileo   Are the gentlemen going to look through or not?

Philosopher   Of course, of course.

Mathematician   Of course.

Pause. Suddenly, **Andrea** *turns and exits stiffly from the room. His mother catches up with him.*

Sarti   What's wrong with you?

Andrea   They're stupid.

Tears himself free and runs away.

Philosopher   Ill-mannered child.

Chamberlain   Highness, gentlemen, can I remind you that the court ball begins in three-quarters of an hour?

Mathematician   Why walk on eggshells? Sooner or later Galileo will have to face facts. His satellites of Jupiter would smash the crystal spheres. It's obvious.

Federonzi   Surprise for you: there are no crystal spheres.

Philosopher   There are – look in any school book.

Federonzi   You need new school books.

Philosopher   Highness, my esteemed colleague and I draw upon the authority of no less a person than Aristotle himself.

Galileo   Who didn't have a telescope.

Mathematician   Indeed not, indeed not.

Philosopher (*grandly*)   If Aristotle is to be dragged through the mud, an authority recognised not only by all the science of the ancient world but also by the great fathers of the church, then further discussion seems to me to be superfluous.

Galileo   The truth is the child of time not of authority. Our ignorance is infinite, let's dig away one spoonful of it! Why try to be so clever when we could finally be a little less stupid! I've had the incredible luck to get my hands on a new instrument that means we can study a tiny point in the universe just a little more closely. Use it.

Philosopher   Your Highness, ladies and gentlemen, I wonder where all this will lead us.

Galileo   It's not our job as scientists to wonder where the truth will take us.

Philosopher (*furious*)   Galileo, the truth may lead us to chaos!

Galileo   Your Highness. Tonight, all over Italy, telescopes are being pointed towards the sky. The moons of Jupiter won't make milk cheaper. But no one's ever seen them before and there they are. And now the ordinary person realises: there's so much to discover if only we open our eyes! They need you to acknowledge that. Italy isn't stirring because of the movement of a few distant stars but because its people have heard that teachings which they thought were immoveable are falling apart. Gentlemen let's not defend old truths.

Federonzi   As teachers, you should be pulling them apart.

Philosopher   We don't need advice in a scientific dispute from your hired hand.

Galileo   Your Highness! My work in the Arsenal of Venice brought me together every day with draughtsmen, builders, instrument makers. These people have shown me a new way. They don't rely on books, they rely on the evidence of their five senses, regardless of where that evidence will take them –

Philosopher   Oho!

Galileo   Today – to find the same curiosity which drove ancient Greece – you have to go to the shipyards.

Chamberlain   Highness, I'm sorry to see that this incredibly educational conversation has become somewhat overextended. His Highness must have a little rest before the ball.

At a signal, the Duke bows to **Galileo**. *The court readies itself quickly to leave.*

Sarti (*stands in the Grand Duke's way and offers him a plate with pastries*)   Something sweet Your Highness?

Galileo (*running after them*)   But all you need to do is look through the telescope!

Chamberlain   On the matter of your assertions, His Highness will seek the opinion of our greatest living astronomer, Christopher Clavius, chief astronomer of the Papal Collegium in Rome.

Five

1616. The Collegium Romanum confirms **Galileo***'s discoveries.*

Scholar   The world has never seen

Fat Prelate   The teacher who sets out to learn.

Thin Monk   Clavius, who ministers God's truth,

All   Agrees with Galileo's proof.

Meeting room of the Collegium Romanum in Rome. Night. In groups, senior priests, monks, scholars. To one side, alone, **Galileo***. A very high-spirited mood. Before the scene begins, we hear roaring laughter.*

Fat Prelate (*holding his sides, laughing*)   Ignorance! Ignorance! If only someone would tell me a fact that the fools didn't believe!

Scholar   Such as: you, Monsignor, are disgusted by the sight of a good meal.

Fat Prelate   Believed, believed. Only sense isn't believed. The devil is real, that's questioned. But the Earth is a pebble rolling in the gutter, that's believed. Sancta simplicitas!

Thin Monk (*playing for laughs*)   I'm giddy. The Earth is spinning too fast. Allow me to hold on to you Professor.

He pretends to sway and holds on to a **Scholar***.*

Scholar (*playing along with it*)   Mother Earth, drunk again, the old crone.

Thin Monk   Stop stop! We're falling off! I said stop!

Second Scholar   Venus is twisted. I can only see half her bottom, help!

A group of monks come together. Laughing, they act as if they were trying to prevent themselves being thrown off a ship in a storm.

Thin Monk   As long as we're not pitched up to the moon. They say, brothers, that its mountain peaks are terribly sharp.

Scholar   Dig your heels in deep.

Thin Monk   And don't look down. I'm feeling dicky.

Fat Prelate   Imagine. In the Collegium Romanum feeling dicky!

Waves of laughter.

From a doorway at the back, come two astrologers from the Collegium. Silence falls.

Thin Monk   Are you still examining this? Scandalous!

Mathematician (*angrily*)   Not us!

Philosopher   How can Christopher Clavius, Italy and the church's greatest astronomer, even consider investigating such a thing!

Fat Prelate   Scandalous!

Mathematician   But he is. Standing there and staring through the tube of the devil.

Very Thin Monk (*comes forward with an open Bible, stabbing frantically with a finger at a verse*)   What does it say here in the scriptures? 'Sun, stand thou still on Gideon and thou moon, in the valley of Ajalon'. How can the sun stand still if it's never moved at all, as this heretic claims? Do the scriptures lie?

Philosopher   There are manifestations which present astronomers with difficulties – but must man understand everything?

Both astronomers exit.

Very Thin Monk   They make the home of the human race just the same as every other planet. They put man, beast, crop and clod into a cart and pull it in circles through an empty heaven. They tell us now there is no Earth or heaven. There's no difference left between what's above and what's below, between eternity and the moment. That we turn to dust, we know. But now they are telling us this: the heavens are dust. There used to be sun and moon and stars and us, living on the Earth. Now there are only stars! One day they will say to us: there aren't man and animals, man is an animal, there are only animals!

Scholar   Galileo, you've let something fall.

Galileo (*who during the above has pulled his stone out of his pocket, played with it and finally dropped it on the floor, bends to pick it up*)   Falling upwards, Monsignor, falling upwards.

Fat Prelate (*turns back*)   A very rude man.

Enter a very **Old Cardinal**, *supported by a monk. Respectfully, everyone makes room for him.*

Old Cardinal   Still in there? Couldn't they have dealt with the whole thing quickly? This Clavius ought to have a grasp of his astronomy! I hear Galileo moves man from the centre of the universe to somewhere on the edge. Which means: he is an enemy of mankind! And as such, he must be dealt with. Man is the crowning glory of all creation, God's greatest and most beloved creature. Would he put such a miraculous piece of work on to a tiny distant star forever spinning away? Would he send his own son to such a place? How can there be people so wicked that they would believe these followers of mathematical calculation? Which of God's creatures would consent to such a thing?

Fat Prelate (*sotto voce*)   The gentleman is amongst us.

Old Cardinal (*to* **Galileo**)   So it's you? You know, I can't see as well as I once could, but I see this: you look remarkably like that man who we once had burned – what was his name?

Monk   Your eminence musn't get excited. The doctor –

Old Cardinal (*shaking him off*)   You seek to degrade the Earth, although you live on it and it gives you everything. It's your own nest and you're fouling it! But whatever happens I won't agree to it. (*He pushes the* **Monk** *aside and begins to walk proudly backwards and forwards.*) I am not some being on some tiny planet that for a little moment turns around somewhere else. I walk on the solid Earth, with a firm step, she is still, she is the centre of the cosmos, I am in the centre and the eye of the creator rests on me and me alone. Around me, fixed on eight crystal spheres, circle the fixed stars and the mighty sun, created to illuminate my world and me, so that God sees me. Everything depends without question on me, God's creation in the centre, the image of God, the eternal and – (*He collapses.*).

Monk   Your Eminence has overexerted himself!

At the same moment, the door at the back opens and, leading his astronomers, there enters the great **Clavius**. *He walks through the room silently and quickly, not looking to either side, and speaks to a monk as he leaves.*

Clavius   It's true.

He exits, followed by the astronomers. The door at the back stays open. Total silence. The very **Old Cardinal** *recovers.*

Old Cardinal   What happened? Did he reach a decision?

Nobody dares to tell him.

Monk   Let us take you home Your Eminence.

They help the old man out. Everybody leaves the room, stunned. A **Little Monk** *from Clavius' investigation panel stops beside* **Galileo**.

Little Monk (*confidentially*)   Galileo, before Father Clavius left he said: Now the theologians will have to see once again how they can square the circles of the heavens. You've won.

Exit.

Galileo (*trying to keep him back*)   Reason has won! Not me, reason!

The **Little Monk** *has already gone.* **Galileo** *goes too. In the doorway, he meets a very tall priest, the* **Cardinal Inquisitor**, *accompanied by an astronomer.* **Galileo** *bows. Before he leaves, he whispers a question to the doorman.*

Who is that?

Secretary (*whispering back*)   His Eminence, the Cardinal Inquisitor.

The astronomer leads the **Cardinal Inquisitor** *to the telescope.*

Six

The Inquisition prohibits the theories of Copernicus (5 March 1616).

In Rome
Galileo visited a cardinal's home
They gave him food to eat and wine to drink
And Galileo wanted just one thing

The house of **Cardinal Bellarmin** *in Rome. A ball is in progress. In the vestibule, where two clerical secretaries are playing chess and writing down what the guests say,* **Galileo** *is greeted with applause by a small group of masked men and women. He is accompanied by his daughter* **Virginia** *and her fiancé* **Ludovico Marsili**.

Ludovico   Ladies and gentlemen.

Virginia   Ludovico, I won't dance with anyone else but you.

Ludovico   Your shoulder strap's coming loose.

Virginia   Father feel my heart.

Galileo (*puts his hand on her heart*)   Still beating.

Virginia   I want to look beautiful.

Galileo   You must or they'll all start wondering again if the Earth turns.

Ludovico   Which it doesn't. (**Galileo** *laughs*.) Rome talks of you alone. But from tonight onwards, they will talk only of your daughter.

Galileo   They say in a Roman spring everyone looks beautiful. Even I resemble an ageing Adonis. (*To the secretaries*.) I'm waiting here for the Cardinal. (*To the young couple*.) Go and play.

Before they go in to the ball at the back, **Virginia** *runs back*.

Virginia   Father, the hairdresser in Via del Trionfo saw to me first and made four other women wait. He knew your name straight away.

Exit.

Galileo (*to the chess-playing secretaries*)   How can you still play the old chess? Cramped. Cramped. Now we play so that the bigger figures move across all the squares. The rook like this – (*He shows them.*) – and the bishop like this – and the queen like this and this. With all that room, you can work out a plan.

The **Very Old Cardinal** *from the previous scene crosses the stage, led by the* **Cardinal**. *He sees* **Galileo**, *walks past him, then turns uncertainly and greets him.* **Galileo** *sits down. From the ballroom we hear choirboys singing the beginning of the famous poem by Lorenzo de Medici.*

'The rose is dead
Petals falling
On cold stone
I understand
Youth's arrogance'

Galileo   Rome. Big celebration?

Secretary   The first since the Plague. Tonight, all of Italy's great families are here.

Second Secretary (*interrupting*)   Their Eminences the Cardinals Bellarmin and Barberini.

Enter **Cardinal Bellarmin** *and* **Barberini**. *They hold masks on sticks in front of their faces: a lamb and a dove.*

Barberini (*pointing at* **Galileo**)   'The sun also ariseth and the sun goeth down and hasteth to his place where he arose'. Thus spake Solomon – what does Galileo say?

Galileo   Eminence, when I was so high (*Indicates with his hand.*) I stood on a boat and called out: the shore's moving. Now I know that the shore is still and the boat is moving.

Barberini   Cunning, cunning. What we see Bellarmin – that the starry sky turns – need not be true. His moons of Jupiter have given our astronomers something to chew on. Sadly I once read something of astronomy. It's a scab that won't heal.

Bellarmin   We must move with the times, Barberini. If this new hypothesis allows for star charts which make our seafarers' navigation easier, then let them use the charts. The only thing that displeases us is teaching which contradicts the scriptures.

He waves greetings into the ballroom.

Galileo   Scripture. 'He that withholdeth corn, the people shall curse him'. Proverbs of Solomon.

Barberini   'A prudent man concealeth knowledge'. Proverbs of Solomon.

Galileo   'A broken spirit drieth the bones'.

Pause.

Doth not wisdom cry?

Barberini   'Can one go upon coals and his feet not be burned?'. Welcome to Rome, my friend. Do you know of its origins? The legend says: two boys received milk and protection from a she wolf. Ever since, the wolf demands payment for her milk. Are you sure my friend that you astronomers don't just want to make astronomy a little easier for yourselves? You think in simple movements as befits your minds. What if it pleaseth God to let his stars move thus?

He draws an extremely complicated path, with erratic speed, in the air.

Galileo   Eminence. If God had made the world thus (*He repeats* **Barberini**'*s path.*) then he would have made our brains thus (*Repeats the same path.*) so it would appear to us as the simplest path. I believe in human reason.

Barberini   I consider human reason to be lacking. He's silent. Too polite to say that I'm lacking.

Bellarmin   Reason, my friend, doesn't go very far. All around us we see lies, crime, folly. Where is truth?

Galileo (*angrily*)   I believe in reason.

Barberini   Don't record this. Friends having a chat about science.

Bellarmin   Consider for a moment the effort that the fathers of the church have made to bring some sense to this brutal world. Consider how viciously men whip their half-naked peasants and the stupidity of those poor people who kiss their master's feet.

Galileo   Disgusting! On the way here I saw –

Bellarmin   We can't understand the meaning of this life. We give up responsibility to a higher power. We carry out another's intentions, we are part of a grand plan. And now – when it comes to the movement of the stars – you would accuse our Maker of being undecided? Whilst you are decided? Is that wise?

Galileo (*preparing to give an explanation*) I am a faithful son of the church –

Barberini   Dreadful. In all innocence, he sets out to prove that God's astronomy is entirely wrong.

Bellarmin   Don't you think that the Maker knows what he has made better than his creature?

Galileo   But if man can misinterpret the movements of the stars then he can also misread the Bible.

Bellarmin   How the Bible is to be read: isn't that for the theologians of the Holy Church to decide?

Galileo *is silent.*

Bellarmin   I see, you're silent. (*He gives a sign to the* **Secretary**.) Galileo this evening the Holy Officium has issued a decree: the teachings of Copernicus – in which the Earth is not at the centre of the cosmos and is on the move – are wrongheaded, ridiculous heresy. I have been given the task of calling on you to renounce his teachings. (*To the* **First Secretary**.) Repeat that.

First Secretary   His eminence Cardinal Bellarmin said to Galileo Galilei: the Holy Officium has issued a decree: the teachings of Copernicus – in which the Earth is not at the centre of the cosmos and is on the move – are wrongheaded, ridiculous heresy. I have been given the task of calling on you to renounce his teachings.

Galileo   What does it mean?

From the ballroom we hear the choirboys singing a further verse of the poem:

'Summer leaves too soon
So pluck the rose in June'

Barberini *signals to* **Galileo** *to be quiet as long as the song lasts. They listen.*

Galileo   But the facts? The astronomers of the Collegium Romanum gave my observations their approval.

Bellarmin   With great satisfaction. They speak of you with nothing but respect.

Galileo   But the moons of Jupiter, the phases of Venus –

Bellarmin   The Officium has come to its conclusion without taking those details into account.

Galileo   So any further scientific research –

Bellarmin   Is assured. So long as it is in line with the views of the church. We may research but we may not draw conclusions. You are free to use the teachings of Copernicus but only as a mathematical hypothesis. Science is the legitimate and dearly beloved daughter of the church. None of us seriously believes that you look to undermine the authority of the church.

Galileo   Authority that's abused withers.

Barberini   Throw out the bathwater, Galileo, not the baby. That's what we're doing. We need you.

Bellarmin   I'm burning with impatience to introduce you to the Officium's mathematician, who holds you in the highest esteem.

Barberini (*taking* **Galileo**'s *other arm*)   And so he changes once again to a lamb. You'd have done better if you'd come in disguise, a wise old teacher. Because I wear this mask today, I'm allowed a little freedom. When I'm wearing my disguise you can hear me say: if God didn't exist, we'd have to make him up. Let's put on our masks again. Poor Galileo has none.

They take **Galileo** *between them and lead him to the ballroom.*

Second Secretary   Have you got that bit where he says he believes in human reason?

Enter the **Cardinal Inquisitor**.

Inquisitor   Has the meeting taken place?

First Secretary   Galileo first entered with his daughter. She has today announced her plan to marry –

The **Inquisitor** *motions for him to move on.*

Galileo then instructed us in a new way of playing chess in which the pieces move all over the board contrary to the rules of the game.

Inquisitor (*waves him on*)   The meeting.

A secretary hands him the transcript and the **Inquisitor** *sits down to skim through it. Two young women in masks cross the stage, they curtsey to the* **Inquisitor**.

One of Them   Who was that?

The Other   The Cardinal Inquisitor.

They giggle. Enter **Virginia**, *looking around searching.*

Inquisitor (*from his corner*)   Yes, my dear?

Virginia (*starts a little, because she didn't see him*)   Oh Your Eminence!

Inquisitor *extends his right hand to her without looking up. She comes closer and kneels to kiss his ring.*

Inquisitor   A wonderful evening! Allow me to congratulate you on your engagement. Your future husband's family is distinguished. Your father needs you. Mathematics is a cold companion, don't you think? A creature of flesh and blood in such surroundings makes all the difference. It's so easy for a great man to get lost in the world of the stars which is so very vast.

Virginia   Your Eminence is very kind. Of such things I understand almost nothing.

Inquisitor   No? (*Laughs.*) In the fisherman's house they don't eat fish. Your father will be tickled when he realises that I've taught you what you know about the stars. (*Leafing through the transcript.*) I see here that your father, a great man, believes our present idea of the importance of the Earth to be somewhat exaggerated. Since ancient times, we have measured the whole of creation as twenty thousand Earth diameters. A pretty big space but small, far too small for our scientists who now say, I understand, that the cosmos is unimaginably wide. A view against which the Holy Officium have taken offence. They're worried: in such a vast space a priest or even a cardinal could get lost. Maybe even the Pope could slip out of sight of the Almighty. Yes, it's comical but still I hope you will continue to watch over your father, who is so precious to us. Possibly I am acquainted with your confessor.

Virginia   Father Christopherus from St Ursula.

Inquisitor   Your father will need you, maybe you can't see it, but he will. Greatness given by God can be a terrible burden. No man is so great that he can't be mentioned in a prayer. But now I'm holding you up. Go in and dance – but don't forget to send Father Christopherus my best wishes.

Virginia *makes a deep curtsey and exits quickly.*

Seven

A conversation.

Galileo read the decree
A young monk came to see him
A poor peasant's son
Searching for wisdom
Searching, searching

In the palace of the Florentine Ambassador to Rome, **Galileo** *listens to the* **Little Monk** *who had whispered the decision of the papal astronomer after the hearing in the Collegium Romanum.*

Galileo   Speak speak! In a monk's habit you can say whatever you like.

Little Monk   Galileo, I've studied mathematics.

Galileo   Which would be a help if it meant that every now and then you admitted that two plus two is four!

Little Monk   I haven't slept for three nights. I didn't know how to reconcile the decree which I read with the moons of Jupiter which I saw. I decided to say early mass and then to come to you.

Galileo   To tell me that Jupiter doesn't have any moons?

Little Monk   No. I've been able to discern the decree's wisdom. It has shown to me that free research is a cause of great danger to humanity and I have decided to renounce astronomy. But I felt it was important that you understand the thinking which can bring even an astronomer to reject further study.

Galileo   If I could just say: I'm familiar with such thinking.

Little Monk   I understand your bitterness. You mean that the church is able to enforce its views with certain exceptional powers.

Galileo   Name them: the instruments of torture.

Little Monk   But I'd like to show you other reasons. Allow me to talk about myself. I grew up the son of peasants. They know everything about olive trees but of anything else almost nothing. As I study the phases of Venus, before me I can see my parents, sitting with my sister at the stove, eating cheese. Above them I see the rafters, which over the centuries have become blackened by smoke, and I see clearly their old hands worn by work and in them little spoons. Their lives are hard but even in their struggle there is a certain hidden pattern. There are routines from the sweeping of the floor to the seasons in the olive groves to the paying of taxes. There's a regularity to the disasters they suffer. My father's back isn't crushed by one blow but slowly in the olive grove every spring, just as steadily as the births which make my mother ever more sexless. They gather strength to carry their baskets sweating up the rocky path, to bear children, yes, to eat, because they feel the constancy, necessity, that comes from watching the soil, with every year its trees newly green, the church, and every Sunday, the word of the Bible. They have been told that the eye of God is upon them, questioning, almost anxious: that all the world's a stage built for them so that they, the actors, can perform their parts well, however small or big. What would my family say if I told them they're on a little lump of rock, endlessly spinning in space around a star, one of many, unimportant! Now what would be the point of their patience, their acceptance of suffering – is there any need or worth in it? Now what would be the point of the scriptures, which have explained and justified everything, the struggle, the patience, the hunger, the servility, and which are now found to be stuffed with error? No, I see them look away, I see them lower their spoons, I see how they feel betrayed, abandoned. So there is no one watching us. Do we have to fend for ourselves as we are – ignorant, old, exhausted? Has no one imagined a part for us to play other than this one, wretched, earthly, here on this tiny planet? Is there no meaning in our suffering, is hunger just a lack of food and not a test of faith; is toil just bending and dragging, not a gift? Do you understand that in the decree I read a mother's noble pity, the soul's great charity?

Galileo   The soul's charity! What you really mean is: the cupboard's bare, the wine's drunk, their lips are dry, so let them kiss the cassock! Why is the cupboard empty? Why in this world is the only rule the rule of the bare cupboard, the order to work until you die? Meanwhile the vineyards flourish beside the fields of wheat. Your peasants are paying for wars led by the representatives of gentle Jesus. Why do they put the Earth in the centre of the universe? So that at the centre of the Earth sits the Pope. That's what it's all about. You're right, it's not about the planets but the peasants. If your family were rich and happy, they'd learn the virtues of being rich and happy. The virtues of exhausted people belong in exhausted fields, and I don't want them. My new water pumps can work far greater miracles than your pointless martyred drudgery. 'Be fruitful and multiply', while the fields are dry and the wars destroy you. You want me to tell your family lies?

Little Monk (*extremely agitated*)   The highest motive compels us to silence: that the souls of the downtrodden find peace.

Galileo   Like to see a gold clock which Cardinal Bellarmin sent me this morning? For leaving your parents' souls in peace, the authorities offer me wine pressed by their bodies' labour. If I agreed to silence it would be for the basest of reasons: easy life, freedom from persecution, blah.

Little Monk   Galileo, I'm a priest.

Galileo   You're also a physicist. And you see the phases of Venus. We can't invent machinery for irrigating the fields without studying the greatest machine of all, the heavenly bodies. The sum of the angles in a triangle can't be altered by decree of the church.

Little Monk   Don't you think that the truth, if it is the truth, will win out, even without us?

Galileo   No. The truth will only win if we win. Reason will triumph only if we reason. You make your peasants sound like the moss on their huts. How could anyone suggest that they will be held back by the sum of the angles on a triangle? But if they don't get moving, learn how to think, even the finest irrigation system will be of no use to them. My God, I see your family's divine patience but where's their divine anger?

Little Monk   They're worn out.

Galileo (*throwing a bundle of manuscripts to the ground*)   My son, are you a physicist? Here are the causes of the ebb and the flow of the oceans of the world. But you musn't read it – understand? Ah! You're reading it already! So you are a physicist?

*The **Little Monk** has buried himself in the paper.*

Galileo An apple from the tree of knowledge. He's swallowing it up. Damned forever but still he swallows, poor pig! You are a physicist! Sometimes I think: I'd let them lock me away in a prison cell fathoms under the earth where it would help me understand the nature of light. And the worst thing of all: whatever I discover, I have to share. Like a lover, like a drunkard, like a traitor. It's nothing more, nothing less than a vice and it means ruin. But how long will I be able to bite my tongue? That is the question.

Little Monk (*pointing to a passage in the papers*)   I don't understand this sentence.

Galileo   I'll explain, I'll explain.

Eight

*After eight years' silence, **Galileo** is encouraged by the accession of a new Pope, who is a scientist, to resume his research in the forbidden field. The sunspots.*

The truth in his trunk
He bit his tongue
He was silent for eight years, such a long time
Truth finds a way

Galileo's *house in Florence. His pupil **Federonzi**, the **Little Monk** and **Andrea Sarti**, now a young man, have gathered for a scientific demonstration. **Galileo** himself is standing reading a book. **Virginia** and **Mrs Sarti** are sewing a trousseau.*

Virginia   It's fun sewing a trousseau. This is for a long dining table, Ludovico enjoys guests. It must be neatly done, his mother checks every stitch. He doesn't approve of Father's books. And neither does Father Christophorus.

Sarti   Well, he hasn't written a book in years.

Virginia   I think he realised that he was wrong. In Rome, a very senior holy father explained astronomy to me. The distances are too great.

Andrea (*writing the tasks for the day up on the board*)   Thursday afternoon – floating bodies – ice again, bucket of water, scales, iron needle, Aristotle.

He fetches the items. The others are reading books.

Sarti   Virginia, I want to talk to you about your wedding. You're still young and you don't have a mother and you have a father who puts bits of ice on water. So I'd advise you not to ask him anything about marriage. But you can't go blindly into something like this. You need to go to a proper astronomer at the university so that he can draw up a horoscope, then you'll know how things will work out. Why are you laughing?

Virginia   I've been there.

Sarti (*very inquisitive*)   And?

Virginia   For three months, I have to be careful because the sun is in Capricorn but then I will have a very favourable ascendant and the clouds will part. As long as I keep an eye on Jupiter, I can go on any journey because I'm a Capricorn.

Sarti   And Ludovico?

Virginia   A Leo. They're supposed to be very sensual.

Pause.

I recognise those footsteps. It's Gaffone, the rector.

Enter **Gaffone**, *the rector from the university.*

Gaffone   Just bringing a book that may interest your father. But for heaven's sake please don't disturb him. Every moment stolen from Galileo is a moment stolen from Italy. I put this book in your hands and then I tiptoe away.

He exits.

Virginia *gives the book to* **Federonzi**.

Galileo   What's it about?

Federonzi   I can't tell. (*Spelling it out*.) 'De maculis in sole'.

Andrea   The sunspots. Another one.

Federonzi, *irritated, gives it to him*.

Listen to the dedication: 'To physic's greatest living authority: Galileo Galilei'.

Galileo *has once again buried himself in his book*.

Andrea   I've read Fabrivius from Holland's treatise on sunspots. He believes that they are clusters of stars passing between the earth and the sun.

Little Monk   That's unlikely isn't it Galileo?

Galileo *doesn't reply*.

Andrea   In Paris and Prague they think that they're sun vapours.

Federonzi   Hmm.

Andrea   Federonzi has his doubts.

Federonzi   Leave me out of it. All I said was 'Hmm'. I'm a lens grinder, I grind lenses and I look through them and see the heavens and where I see 'spots' you see 'maculis'. How can I have doubts? I can't read these books, they're in Latin.

In his anger, he waves the scales around. One of the dishes falls to the ground. **Galileo** *goes over and silently picks it up.*

Little Monk   Doubting is happiness. I wonder.

Andrea   For the last two weeks every time it's sunny I've climbed up to the attic. There's a little ray of light which shines through the gaps in the shingles. On a piece of paper, you can catch an image of the sun upside down. I saw a spot, big as a fly, formless as a small cloud. It moved. Why don't we study the spots?

Galileo   Because we're working on floating bodies.

Andrea   Mother's got washing baskets full of letters. All Europe wants to know your opinion. Your reputation's grown so vast you can't be silent.

Galileo   Rome's allowed my reputation to grow because I've stayed silent.

Federonzi   But you can't stay silent any longer.

Galileo   And I won't be a hog stuck on a burning bonfire to roast.

Andrea   So you think the spots have got something to do with the other stuff?

Galileo *doesn't reply.*

Andrea   All right, we'll stick with the bits of ice; that can't harm you.

Galileo   Exactly. Our thesis Andrea!

Andrea   With regards to floating, we propose that it is not the shape of the body that matters but whether it is lighter or heavier than water.

Galileo   What does Aristotle say?

Little Monk   'Discus latus platique'.

Galileo   Translate, translate!

Little Monk   A broad, flat disc of ice will float on water whereas an iron needle will sink.

Galileo   According to Aristotle why doesn't the ice sink?

Little Monk   Because it's wide and flat and as such unable to divide the water.

Galileo   Good.

He picks up a piece of ice and puts it in the bucket.

Now I push the ice hard down to the bottom of the bucket. I remove the pressure of my hands. And what happens?

Little Monk   It comes back to the surface.

Galileo   Correct. Seemingly it separates the water as it rises.

Andrea   But why does it float at all? Ice is heavier than water, it's condensed water.

Galileo   What if it was diluted water?

Andrea   It must be lighter than water or it wouldn't float.

Galileo   Aha.

Andrea   Just like an iron needle doesn't float. Everything that's lighter than water floats, everything that's heavier sinks. Quod erat demonstrandum.

Galileo   Andrea, you must learn to think methodically. Give me the iron needle. A sheet of paper. Is iron heavier than water?

Andrea   Yes.

Galileo *lays the needle on the sheet of paper and then gently slides the needle on the surface of the water. Pause.*

Galileo   What's happened?

Federonzi   The needle is floating! Great Aristotle – they never tested you!

They laugh.

Galileo   In science one of the main causes of poverty is imagined wealth. The aim is not to open the door to infinite wisdom but to limit infinite error. Write up our observations.

Virginia   What is it?

Sarti   Every time they laugh, I shudder. I think: what's caused the laughter?

Virginia   Father says: the churchman has his ringing bell and the physicist has his laughter.

Sarti   At least he doesn't look through his tube any more. That was worse.

Virginia   Now he's only putting bits of ice in water, nothing bad can come from that.

Sarti   I'm not so sure.

Enter **Ludovico Marsili** *in travelling clothes, followed by a servant carrying luggage.* **Virginia** *runs up to him and embraces him.*

Virginia   Why didn't you write and say you were coming?

Ludovico   I was nearby visiting our vineyards in Bucciole and I couldn't resist you.

Galileo (*as if short-sighted*)   Who is it?

Virginia   Ludovico.

Little Monk   Can't you see him?

Galileo   Oh yes, Ludovico. (*He goes up to him.*) How are the horses?

Ludovico   Doing well, sir.

Galileo   Sarti, we'll celebrate. Bring a jug of the Sicilian wine, the old one.

Sarti *exits with* **Andrea**.

Ludovico   You look pale. Life in the country will suit you. Mother expects you in September.

Virginia   Wait – I'll show you my wedding dress!

Virginia *runs out.*

Galileo   Sit down.

Ludovico   What are you working on at the moment?

Galileo   Dull stuff, routine. Did you come through Rome?

Ludovico   Mother says well done on being so tactful about all this Dutch sunspot craze.

Galileo (*drily*)   Thanks.

Sarti *and* **Andrea** *bring in wine and glasses. They all gather round the table.*

Ludovico   Rome's already got a topic for February's gossip: Father Christopher Clavius has expressed his fear that these sunspots will set off the whole Earth around the sun nonsense again.

Andrea   Nothing to worry about.

Galileo   Any other snatches of news from the Holy City apart from hopes of me sinning anew?

Ludovico   You know of course that the Holy Father is dying?

Little Monk   Oh.

Galileo   Who's talked of as the successor?

Ludovico   Most people say Barberini.

Galileo   Barberini.

Andrea   Galileo knows Barberini.

Little Monk   Cardinal Barberini is a mathematician.

Federonzi   A scientist on the Papal Throne!

Galileo   So now they need men like Barberini who've read a bit of mathematics. Things are on the move. Federonzi, we'll live to see the day when we don't have to glance over our shoulders before we say: two twos are four. (*To* **Ludovico**.) A good wine. What do you think?

Ludovico   It's good.

Galileo   I know the vineyard. A steep, stony hillside, the grape almost blue. But I love its wine.

Ludovico   Yes, sir.

Galileo   It has little shadows in it. Almost sweet. You have to admit, almost. Andrea clear all this stuff away – ice, bucket, needle. I enjoy the body's pleasures. I have no time for those cowardly souls who call them weaknesses. I say: pleasure is an achievement.

Little Monk   What are you doing?

Federonzi   It's starting again: the great noise of the Earth spinning around the sun.

Andrea (*humming*)

The Bible says the Earth stands still
A fact that every learned doctor proves
The Pope decrees it must not, will
Not spin – and yet it does, it moves!

Andrea, **Federonzi** and the **Little Monk** *hurry to the experiment table and clear it.*

Andrea   Maybe we'll discover that the sun turns too. How would you like that Marsili?

Ludovico   What is all this?

Sarti   Are you going to start again with the devil's work?

Galileo   So that's why your mother sent you. Barberini is on the up! Science will be a passion, research bliss. Clavius is right: these sunspots fascinate me. Does my wine taste good Ludovico?

Ludovico   As I said sir.

Galileo   Does it really taste good?

Ludovico (*stiffly*)   It tastes good.

Galileo   So you'd take a man's wine or his daughter and not demand that he abandons his calling? What's my astronomy got to do with my daughter? The phases of Venus won't change her arse.

Sarti   Mind your tongue. I'm going to fetch Virginia straight away.

Ludovico (*holding her back*)   Marriages in families such as mine are not based only on matters sexual.

Galileo   They restrained you from marrying my daughter for eight years while I was on probation?

Ludovico   My wife will also be a public figure in the congregation of our local church.

Galileo   And you think that the peasants will take into account the saintliness of their landlady before they decide to pay their rents?

Ludovico   To some degree.

Galileo   Andrea, Fulganzio, fetch the brass mirror and the screen! We'll catch the sun on that to spare our eyes. Your method, Andrea.

Andrea *and the* **Little Monk** *fetch the mirror and the screen.*

Ludovico   In Rome, you gave your word that you wouldn't get caught up in this Earth moves round the sun thing.

Galileo   That was then. We had a reactionary Pope.

Sarti   Had! And His Holiness not yet dead!

Galileo   As good as, as good as. Place a grid of squares over the screen. We'll proceed methodically and then we can answer their letters can't we Andrea?

Sarti   'As good as'! He weighs that lump of ice fifty times but when it's something that suits him, he believes it blindly.

They set up the screen.

Ludovico   Should His Holiness die, Galileo, the next Pope, whoever it may be and however greatly he may love science, he will also have to bear in mind how great will be the love felt for him by our country's noblest families.

Little Monk   God made the physical world, Ludovico; God made the human brain; God will allow physics.

Sarti   Galileo, now it's my turn to tell you something. I've seen my boy drawn in to these 'experiments' and 'theories' and 'observations' and I've been unable to stop him. You set yourself up against the authorities and they've given you your warning. The most eminent cardinals have steered you like a sick horse. It worked for a while but two months ago I caught you at it again, starting up your observations in secret. In the attic! I didn't say anything but I knew. I rushed out and lit a candle to St Joseph. It was all too much for me. If I have to give up my eternal soul because I've served a heretic, that's my business, but you have no right to trample your own daughter's happiness under your heavy feet!

Galileo (*annoyed*)   Bring the telescope!

Ludovico   Giuseppe, take my luggage back to the coach.

Exit servant.

Sarti   This will kill her! You can tell her yourself!

Ludovico   I see you've started already. Galileo, Mother and I spend three-quarters of the year on our estate in the Campagna and I can assure you that your papers on Jupiter and its moons don't trouble our peasants. Their work in the fields is too hard. But it would trouble them to discover that petty assaults upon holy doctrine now go unpunished. Remember that these poor unfortunates, more beast than man, get everything muddled. And they really are animals. A rumour goes round – a pear has been seen on an apple tree – and they run from the fields to gossip.

Galileo (*interested*)   Yes?

Ludovico   Animals. Up they come to the house to complain about some triviality and Mother is compelled to have a dog flayed before them, the only thing that reminds them of law and decency and good manners. Galileo, occasionally you look from a carriage at bountiful fields of maize, without thinking you eat our olives and our cheese, but you have no idea what effort, what leadership it costs to make them grow.

Galileo   Young man, I never eat olives without thinking. (*Angrily.*) You're holding me up. (*Calls out.*) Where's the telescope?

Andrea   Are you ready?

Galileo   It's not just the dogs you beat to keep them in their place is it Marsili?

Ludovico   Galileo, you have a wonderful brain. A shame.

Little Monk (*surprised*)   He's threatening you.

Galileo   Yes. I might inspire his peasants to think new thoughts. And his servants and his stewards.

Federonzi   How? None of them reads Latin.

Galileo   I could write in the people's language. New thoughts need people who work with their hands. Who else needs to know where everything comes from? Those who only see the bread on the table don't want to know how it was baked – they'd rather thank God than the baker. But those who make the bread, they know that nothing moves which isn't moved. Your sister at the olive press, Fulganzio, won't be so surprised – she may well laugh – when she hears that the sun isn't a golden coat of arms but a lever: the Earth moves because the sun moves it.

Ludovico   You'll always be a slave to your obsessions. Send my apologies to Virginia: I think it's best if I don't see her.

Galileo   Any time you need the dowry, it's yours.

Ludovico   Good day.

He goes.

Andrea   All the best to the Marsilis!

Federonzi   Who tell the Earth: stand still so that my castles don't fall.

Galileo   So now we begin to study these spots on the sun, which interest us, at our own risk and without relying on the protection of a new Pope.

Andrea   But with full confidence that we can prove the rotation of the sun.

Galileo   With some confidence that we can prove the rotation of the sun. My aim is not to prove that I've been right all along but to test if I am. I say: abandon all hope, you who begin to observe. Perhaps they're clouds, perhaps they're spots but before we assume that they are spots, which would suit us, let us rather assume that they are the tails of fish. We'll approach the observation of the sun with an unswerving determination to prove that the Earth stands still. And only when we've failed, totally broken, wounded and in deep despair, only then shall we begin to ask if we weren't right after all and maybe the Earth does move.

He sets up the brass mirror.

Little Monk   I knew that you'd already begun working. I knew it when you couldn't see Ludovico Marsili.

*They begin their observations. As the flaming image of the sun appears on the screen, **Virginia** comes running, wearing her wedding dress.*

Virginia   Father, you sent him away!

*She faints. **Andrea** and the **Little Monk** hurry to her.*

Galileo   Take the cloth off the telescope and point it at the sun.

Nine

*A decade passes: **Galileo**'s teaching spreads amongst the people. Everywhere, writers of pamphlets and singers of ballads pass on the new ideas. During the carnivals of 1632, many Italian cities choose astronomy as the theme for their guild processions.*

Ballad Singer
  Day of creation
  God said to the sun:
  'Miss, here's a candle
  Hold it in your hand
  Spin around the Earth'

What he wanted was
Universal order
Greatest above in
Heaven and on Earth

But Galileo
Threw down the Bible
Looked in his tube, said:
'Stay where you are Sun
Let the mistress Earth
Spin around her maid'

Think I'm joking? The servants are getting bolder every day.
Better face it: who doesn't want to be their own master?

The serf is asleep
The maid answers back
The butcher's dog's fat
No choirboy at mass

Don't mess with the Bible! Rope isn't thick enough around
   our necks – it's breaking.
Better face it: who doesn't want to be their own master?

Good people – here's the future as seen by Galileo:

Farmer takes his scythe
Cuts down the landlord
His wife gives her kids
Milk meant for the priest

Rope isn't thick enough around our necks – it's breaking.
Better face it: who doesn't want to be their own master?

Singer's Wife
If stars are moving
Then maybe I can
Find a new lover
Meet a man who's got –

Singer

That's enough! Take the muzzle off the bitch and it bites!
Who doesn't want to be their own master?

Both

All you who suffer on this Earth
Hear Galileo's teaching
Obey no longer
And we'll grow stronger
Who doesn't want to be their own master?

Singer

And now Galileo's great discovery: the Earth spins round
the sun!

Drumbeat. The woman carries a rough image of the sun and the child, carrying a pumpkin above its head to represent the Earth, circles around the woman.

Voice   The procession!

Two men pull a little cart. On a ridiculous throne sits 'the Duke of Florence', dressed in sacking, a cardboard crown, looking through a telescope. Above the throne, a sign reads 'LOOKING FOR TROUBLE'.

Four masked men march on carrying a heavy sheet. They stop and toss a dummy representing a cardinal up in the air. A dwarf stands to one side with a sign which reads 'A NEW AGE'.

In the crowd a beggar rises up on his crutches, makes a stamping dance until he falls down.

*Enter an oversized dummy of **Galileo**, who bows to the crowd. In front of the dummy, a child carries a huge Bible open with the pages crossed out.*

Singer   Galileo Galilei – the breaker of Bibles!

Huge laughter from the crowd.

Ten

The Inquisition summons the world-famous scientist to Rome.

It's hot below, it's cool on high
The street is busy, the court is quiet

Antechamber and staircase in the palace of the Medici in Florence.
Galileo *and* **Virginia** *wait to be received by the* **Grand Duke**.

Virginia   It's taking a long time.

Galileo   Yes.

Virginia   There he is again, that monk who followed us here.

She points out someone who walks past without looking at them.

Galileo *(whose sight has faded)*   I don't know him.

Virginia   But I've seen him several times in the last few days. He frightens me.

Galileo   Nonsense. We're in Florence not with Corsican pirates.

Virginia   Here's the Rector.

Galileo   Now he is frightening. Once he traps you in conversation you're there for hours.

Gaffone, *Rector of the University, comes down the stairs. He is visibly shocked when he sees* **Galileo**, *and walks stiffly past, his head turned awkwardly away.*

Galileo   What's got into him? My eyes are bad again today. Did he acknowledge us?

Virginia   Barely. What does it say in your book? Is it possible that they think it's heresy?

Galileo   You spend too much time in church. Getting up early, running off to mass, it's bad for your complexion. You say prayers for me don't you?

Virginia   Here's Vanni, the iron founder, you designed his smelting plant. Remember – thank him for the quails.

A man is coming down the stairs.

Vanni   Enjoy the quails Galileo?

Galileo   Vanni the quails were excellent. Many thanks.

Vanni   They're talking about you up there. Saying you're responsible for all the anti-Bible pamphlets that are on sale everywhere.

Galileo   I don't know anything about pamphlets. My favourite reading is Homer and the Bible.

Vanni   I want to say: the manufacturers are on your side. I don't know much about the movement of the stars but you're the man who fights for the freedom to teach new ideas. That mechanical cultivator from Germany you told me about. The Dutch canals. Same people holding you back won't allow research doctors in Bologna to dissect corpses. Do you know that in London and Amsterdam they now have stock exchanges? And business schools. Papers printed regularly with the latest news. And we're not even free to make a profit. They're against iron foundries because they say too many workers in one place breeds immorality! I stand right beside you Galileo. If they ever try to do anything to you, remember: you have friends in the business community.

Galileo   As far as I know, no one has the intention of doing anything to me.

Vanni   No?

Galileo   No.

Vanni   I think you'd be better off in Venice. Fewer monks. There, you could start the fight back. I've got a coach and horses.

Galileo   I can't picture myself as a refugee. I value my comfort.

Vanni   From what I heard up there, I think they'd rather that you weren't in Florence just now.

Galileo   Nonsense. The Grand Duke is my pupil and the Pope himself would put a stop to any trap set for me.

Vanni   Seems to me: you can't tell your friends from your enemies.

Galileo   I can tell the powerful from the powerless.

He breaks away.

Vanni   Alright then. I wish you luck.

Exit **Vanni**.

Galileo (*back with* **Virginia**)   I've written a book about the mechanics of the cosmos, that's all. What they make of it has nothing to do with me.

Virginia (*softly*)   Did the Grand Duke actually summon you today?

Galileo   No but I've asked to be announced. He must want the book, he paid for it.

Virginia   Can't you leave the book here? You're wasting your time.

Galileo   Maybe I'll take up Sagredo's invitation. Go to Padua for a few weeks. My health's not so good.

Virginia   You can't live without your books.

Galileo   I could take some of that Sicilian wine.

Virginia   The court still owes you three months' salary. They won't send it on.

Galileo   True.

The **Cardinal Inquisitor** *comes down the stairs.*

Virginia   The Cardinal Inquisitor.

Passing, he bows low to **Galileo**.

Virginia   Father, why is the Cardinal Inquisitor in Florence?

Galileo   I don't know. He behaved with respect.

Second Lady (*calls out*)   His Highness, the Grand Duke!

Cosimo de Medici *comes down the stairs.* **Galileo** *approaches him.* **Cosimo** *stops, slightly embarrassed.*

Galileo   Your Highness, my dialogues on the two great world systems –

Cosimo   Aha, aha. How are your eyes?

Galileo   Not at their best, Your Highness. If you will allow me, my book –

Cosimo   I'm worried about your eyes. Really I am. Maybe you've been overdoing it with the telescope?

He walks on without taking the book.

Galileo   He didn't take the book, did he?

Virginia   Father, I'm frightened.

Galileo   Keep your feelings hidden. We won't go home. I've arranged a wagon with empty barrels ready to carry us away.

Virginia   You knew . . .

Galileo   Don't look back.

High Official (*coming down the stairs*)   Galileo, it is my duty to inform you that the court of Florence is no longer in a position to deny the request of the Holy Inquisition to examine you in Rome. The coach of the Holy Inquisition is waiting.

Eleven

Room in the Vatican. **Pope Urban VIII** (*formerly* **Cardinal Barberini**) *has received the* **Cardinal Inquisitor**. *During the audience, he is being dressed in his robes. Outside the sound of many feet shuffling.*

Pope (*very loud*)   No! No! No!

Inquisitor   So Your Holiness wants me to inform the doctors of all faculties who are assembled here, the representatives of all the holy orders and the entire priesthood – who come, with a child's faith in God's word as set down in the scriptures, to hear Your Holiness confirm that faith – that the scriptures can no longer be regarded as true?

Pope   I won't say 2 x 2 = 5. No!

Inquisitor   It's not the multiplications themselves. A terrible restlessness has come into the world. Unrest in the minds of men is pressed on to the unmoving Earth. They shout: 'It's the maths that makes me do it! The numbers!' But where do the numbers come from? From doubt. These people doubt everything. Can we base a society on 'possibly' and leave behind 'I believe'? 'You're my master – possibly'. 'Your house, your wife – possibly'. Your Holiness' love of art – to which we owe many beautiful collections – is mocked in graffiti on the walls of Rome. 'What the Barbarians didn't sack, the Barberinis now grab'. And elsewhere? Your Holiness' foreign policy is – misunderstood. Plague, war, Reformation are tearing all Christendom into scraps – and now those maggots, the mathematicians, point their telescopes to the heavens and tell the world that even there, in the sphere where you should hold sway, you are defeated. You have to ask yourself: why this sudden interest in an obscure discipline like astronomy? There's nobody left in Italy – even the stable boys – thanks to the teachings of this malicious Florentine – who isn't chattering about the phases of Venus. What will happen if these people – weak in spirit, inclined to excess – were to believe, as this madman impels them, in no higher authority than their own common sense? Ever since they've set sail across the ocean – nothing wrong with that – they've put faith in a compass before God. Machines like Galileo's they say perform miracles. So they don't need God any more. They say there's no Above, no

Below. No longer needed. If the shuttle weaves by itself and the zither plucks its own strings, then the master needs no apprentices, the ruler needs no servants. That's what they're thinking. This devil knows what he's doing when he writes his astronomy, not in Latin, but in the tongue of the fishwife and the wool merchant.

Pope   That's in very bad taste: I'll mention it to him. The shuffling is unnerving me. It's very distracting.

Inquisitor   Holiness, perhaps they speak more eloquently than I can. Must they all leave here with doubt in their hearts?

Pope   This man is the greatest physicist of the age, the light of Italy – you must not use a heavy hand.

Inquisitor   In practice, we wouldn't have to go very far with him. He's a man of the flesh. He would give way immediately.

Pope   He loves pleasure more than any man I've met. His thought is sensual. An old wine or a new thought – he can't say no. I don't want hard facts to be condemned. 'Here's the Church, there's Reason!'. I allowed him to write his book as long as the final words were not of science but faith. He kept to that.

Inquisitor   In his book a stupid man – representing the views of Aristotle – argues with a clever man – who of course puts forth the views of Galileo. And who is it that speaks the final words? Not the clever man.

Pope   That is offensive. The stamping in the corridors really is intolerable. Is the whole world coming here?

Inquisitor   Its best part.

*The **Pope** is now in full robes.*

Pope   The very most that may be done is to show him the instruments.

Inquisitor   That will be enough Holiness. Galileo
understands instruments.

Twelve

*On 22 June 1633, before the Inquisition, Galileo Galilei recants his
teaching about the movement of the earth.*

It was one short day in June
But what a day for me and you
Out of the darkness reason should have come
But he denied the Earth moves round the sun

In the palace of the Florentine Ambassador in Rome. **Galileo***'s
pupils are waiting for news. The* **Little Monk** *and* **Federonzi** *play
new chess with its sweeping movements. In the corner* **Virginia**
kneels and says her hail marys.

Little Monk   The Pope didn't receive him. No more
scientific discussion.

Federonzi   His last hope. It was true what he said to him
years ago in Rome, when he was still Cardinal Barberini: 'We
need you'. Now they've got him.

Andrea   They'll destroy him. The Dialogues will never be
finished.

Federonzi (*looks at him furtively*)   You think so?

Andrea   Because he'll never recant.

Pause.

Little Monk   When you can't sleep at night your mind
dwells on little details. Last night I kept thinking: I wonder if
they'll let him keep his stone, the one he always carries in his
pocket. His stone of proof.

Federonzi   Where they're taking him, there's no pockets.

Andrea (*shouts*)   They wouldn't dare! And even if they do that to him, he won't recant. 'He who knows not the truth is a fool but he who knows it and calls it a lie is a criminal'.

Federonzi   I don't think he will either, and I wouldn't want to live if he did, but they have force.

Andrea   You can't achieve everything by force.

Federonzi   Maybe not.

Andrea (*of* **Virginia**)   She's praying that he'll recant.

Federonzi   Leave her alone. She lost her senses after they spoke to her. They summoned her Father Confessor from Florence.

Enter **Cosimo** *from the Grand Duke's palace in Florence.*

Person   Galileo will be here soon. He may be in need of a bed.

Federonzi   He's been released?

Person   It is expected that at five o'cock, in a session of the Inquisition, Galileo will recant. The great bell of St Mark's will be rung and the words of recantation will be read in public.

Andrea   I don't believe it.

Person   Due to the great throng on the streets, Galileo will be brought to the garden gate here at the back of the palace.

Exit.

Andrea (*suddenly loud*)   The moon is an Earth and has no light of its own. Just as Venus has no light of its own and like the Earth revolves around the sun. And four moons revolve around the planet Jupiter which is not attached to any crystal sphere. And the sun is at the centre of the universe and fixed and the Earth is not at the centre and is not fixed. And he's the one who has shown this to us.

Little Monk   And with force you cannot make unseen what has already been seen.

Silence.

Federonzi (*looks at the sundial in the garden.*)   Five o'clock.

Virginia *prays louder.*

Andrea   I can't wait any longer. They are murdering the truth.

He blocks up his ears, as does the **Little Monk**. *But the bell is not rung. After a pause, filled by* **Virginia**'s *murmured prayers,* **Federonzi** *shakes his head to say 'No'. The others let their hands drop.*

Federonzi (*hoarsely*)   Nothing. Three minutes past five.

Andrea   He's standing firm.

Little Monk   He's not recanting.

Federonzi   Oh we happy people!

They embrace. They are overcome with joy.

Andrea   So – they didn't win with force. It isn't everything! So – stupidity is vanquished, it's not invincible! So – Man is not afraid of death!

Federonzi   Now it's really begun: the age of science. This is the hour when it's born. Just think – if he'd recanted!

Little Monk   I didn't say it but I was so stuffed with fear. Oh, I of little faith!

Kneels down, weeping.

Lord, I thank thee!

Andrea   Today everything has changed. Man, tortured mankind, lifts up its head and says: I can live. So much is won when a single man stands up and says No!

At this moment the bell of St Mark's begins to toll. All stand rigid.

Virginia (*stands up*)   The bell of St Mark's. He is not damned!

From the street outside we can hear the crier reading out **Galileo**'s *recantation.*

Crier's Voice   'I Galileo Galilei teacher of mathematics and physics at the University of Florence, renounce that which I have taught, that the sun is the centre of the universe and immoveable and that the Earth is not the centre and not immoveable. I renounce, detest and curse with sincere heart and true faith all these lies and heresies as well as every other falsehood and opinion which is against the teachings of the Holy Church.'

It grows dark.

When it grows light again, the bell is still tolling and then stops. **Virginia** *has gone.* **Galileo**'s *pupils are still there.*

Federonzi   He never paid you properly for your work. Andrea you couldn't buy a pair of trousers or publish your own work. And you Little Monk you suffered because you were working 'for science'.

Andrea (*loudly*)   Unhappy the land that has no heroes!

Galileo *has entered, completely altered by the trial, almost unrecognisable. He has heard* **Andrea**'s *exclamation. For several moments he waits in the doorway for a greeting. When no one comes, since his pupils shrink away from him, he walks forwards, uncertain because of his failing sight, where he finds a stool and sits down.*

Andrea   I can't look at him. Make him leave.

Federonzi   Calm.

Andrea (*shouts at* **Galileo**)   Wine guzzler! Quail stuffer! Saved your own flesh?

Sits down.

I feel ill.

Galileo   Give him a glass of water.

*The **Little Monk** fetches **Andrea** a glass of water from outside.
The others take no notice of **Galileo**, who sits on the stool listening.
From far off, the voice of the crier can be heard again.*

Andrea   I can walk now if you help me.

*They help him to the door. At this moment **Galileo** starts to speak.*

Galileo   No. Unhappy the land that is in need of heroes.

Thirteen

*1633–1642 **Galileo** lives in a house in the country near Florence,
a prisoner of the Inquisition until his death. The 'discorsi'.*

Sixteen hundred and thirty-three to
Sixteen hundred and forty-two
Galileo is a prisoner of the church
Until his death

*A large room with table, leather chair and globe. **Galileo**, now old
and half blind, is experimenting carefully with a small wooden ball
on a curved wooden track. In the antechamber a **Monk** is on watch.
A knock at the door. The **Monk** opens it and a **Peasant** enters,
carrying two plucked geese. **Virginia** comes out of the kitchen. She is
now about forty.*

Peasant   I was told: deliver these.

Virginia   Who are they from? I didn't order goose.

Peasant   Been told to say: from someone who is passing
through.

Exits.

Virginia *looks at the geese, astonished. The **Monk** takes them from
her and examines them suspiciously. Then, satisfied, he returns them
and she carries them by their necks to **Galileo** in the large room.*

Virginia   Somebody passing through has sent a gift.

Galileo   What is it?

Virginia   Can't you see?

Galileo   No.

She comes over.

Geese. No name?

Virginia   No.

Galileo (*taking one of the geese*)   Heavy. Fancy a bit of that.

Virginia   You can't be hungry again already. You just had supper. Is there something wrong with your eyes again? You should have seen them from your chair.

Galileo   You're standing in the shadows.

Virginia   I'm not standing in the shadows.

She carries the geese out.

Galileo   Cook them with thyme and apple.

Virginia (*to the* **Monk**)   We must send for the eye doctor. Father couldn't see the geese from his chair.

Monk   I need to get permission from Monsignor Carpula. Has he been doing his own writing again?

Virginia   No. He's been dictating his book to me. You've got pages 131 and 132 and they're the last.

Monk   He's an old fox.

Virginia   He's not breaking the rules. He has genuinely repented. I'm watching him.

She gives him the geese.

Tell the kitchen: roast the livers with an apple and an onion.

She goes back to the big room.

And now we'll take care of those eyes and leave the ball alone immediately and dictate a little bit more of our weekly letter to the Archbishop.

Galileo I don't feel well enough. Read me some Horace.

Virginia Only last week Monsignor Carpula who we have so much to thank for – just the other day, more vegetables – he told me that the Archbishop asks every time if you like the meditations and quotations he sends you.

She has sat down to take dictation.

Galileo Where was I?

Virginia Paragraph four: Regarding the position taken by the Holy Church on the unrest in the Arsenal of Venice, I agree entirely with the position taken by Cardinal Spoletti towards the mutinous rope makers . . .

Galileo (*dictates*) I agree entirely with the position taken by Cardinal Spoletti towards the mutinous rope makers that it is better to distribute soup in the name of Christian charity than it is to pay them any more for their hawsers and bell ropes. For it is their faith which we must reward and not their greed. Paul the Apostle says: charity never faileth. How's that?

Virginia It's brilliant Father.

Galileo You don't think they might read some irony?

Virginia The Archbishop will be so pleased.

Galileo I'll let you be the judge of that. What's next?

Virginia A beautiful saying: 'When I am weak, then am I strong'.

Galileo No comment. Next.

Virginia 'And to know the love of Christ which passeth knowledge'. Ephesians iii 19.

Galileo I thank Your Eminence especially for the wonderful text from the Epistle to the Ephesians. Inspired by this I found this morning in our inimitable Imatio the following: (*He quotes by heart.*) 'He to whom the eternal word speaketh is free from many questions'. May I take this opportunity to speak of myself? Still I'm reproached because once I wrote a book about the heavenly bodies in the language of the market place. By doing this, I never intended to suggest or support books on subjects of far more importance such as theology being written in the slang of the spaghetti merchants. That sacred matters should be understood so cheaply is something I have no wish for. The Latin of the pulpit, which protects the eternal truth of the church from the questions of the ignorant awakens trust when – No cross that out.

Virginia   All of it?

Galileo   Everything after 'spaghetti merchants'.

Virginia *goes to the ante-chamber. The* **Monk** *opens up. It is* **Andrea Sarti**. *He is now a middle-aged man.*

Andrea   Good evening. I'm about to leave Italy, scientific research in Holland and I've been asked to visit him on my way through, so that I can give them news of him.

Virginia   I don't know whether he'll see you. You've never been.

Andrea   Ask him.

Galileo *has recognised the voice. He sits unmoving.* **Virginia** *goes in to him.*

Galileo   Is it Andrea?

Virginia   Shall I send him away?

Galileo (*after a pause*)   Let him in.

Virginia *shows* **Andrea** *in.*

Virginia (*to the* **Monk**)   He's harmless. Once he was his pupil. So now he's his enemy.

Galileo   Leave me alone with him, Virginia.

Virginia   I want to hear his news.

She sits down.

Andrea (*coldly*) How are you?

Galileo Come closer. What are you working on? I hear it's to do with hydraulics.

Andrea Fabricius in Amsterdam has requested that I ask after your health.

Pause.

Galileo I'm well. I'm given every attention.

Andrea I'm pleased that I can report that your health is good.

Galileo Fabricius will be pleased. And tell him that I live in befitting comfort. Such is the depth of my repentance that my superiors allow me modest scientific study under clerical control.

Andrea Yes. We heard that the church is content. Your total submission has been effective. In Italy, as the authorities have noted with satisfaction, no further work with new ideas has been published since you recanted.

Galileo (*listening*) Sadly there are countries which refuse the protection of the church. I worry that there the condemned teachings may be spread.

Andrea There too, because you recanted, there's been a setback that the church finds gratifying.

Galileo Really?

Pause.

Nothing from Descartes? From Paris?

Andrea Yes. When he heard you'd recanted, he stuffed his thesis on the nature of light into a drawer.

Long pause.

Galileo I am anxious about certain scientific friends who I led on to the path of error. Have they been enlightened by my recantation?

Andrea   Federonzi is grinding lenses again in some shop in Milan. Fulganzio, our little monk, has given up research and returned to the embrace of the church.

Galileo   The authorities hope for my spiritual recovery. I'm doing better than expected.

Andrea   Well.

Virginia   May God be praised.

Galileo (*sharply*)   See to the geese, Virginia.

Virginia *leaves angrily. As she goes past, the* **Monk** *speaks to her.*

Monk   I don't trust that one.

Virginia   He's harmless. You heard them. (*As she leaves.*) Some fresh goat's cheese has just arrived.

The **Monk** *follows her out.*

Andrea   I'll travel through the night so that I can cross the border tomorrow morning. Can I go?

Galileo   I don't know why you came here Sarti. To upset me? Since I came here, I've lived carefully, thought carefully. But I have my relapses.

Andrea   I don't want to agitate you Galileo.

Galileo   Barberini called it the itch. He was never quite free of it himself. I've been writing again.

Andrea   Yes?

Galileo   I've finished the Discorsi.

Andrea   Discourses Between Two New Sciences: Mechanics and the Laws of Falling Bodies?

Galileo   They give us paper, pens. They're not fools. They know you can't break a bad habit in one day. They protect me from any unfortunate consequences by locking it away, page by page.

Andrea   They're making you plough water! The Discorsi in the hands of the monks! Two new sciences as good as lost!

Galileo   It will please you and no doubt a few others that I have risked the last pathetic remains of ease of mind by making a copy, behind – as it were – my own back, using up the last ounce of light of every clear night for the last six months.

Andrea   You made a copy?

Galileo   To date, my vanity has not allowed for its destruction.

Andrea   Where is it?

Galileo   Inside the globe. If you risk taking it to Holland you will of course have to assume full responsibility. You will have bought it from someone who has access to the original in the Holy Officium.

Andrea *has gone to the globe. He takes out the copy.*

Andrea   The Discorsi.

He leafs through the manuscript.

Andrea   My project is to found a new science treating a very old subject, motion.

Galileo   I had to do something, pass the time.

Andrea   A new science.

Galileo   Stuff it under your coat.

Andrea   And we thought you were a traitor! I shouted it the loudest!

Galileo   And you were right. I taught you science and denied the truth.

Andrea   This changes everything. Everything.

Galileo   Really?

Andrea   You hid the truth. From the enemy. Even in the field of ethics you're centuries ahead of us.

Galileo   Do you mind unpicking that Andrea?

Andrea   The man on the street said – as we did – 'He'll die before he recants'. You returned: 'I have recanted but I shall live'. 'Your hands are bloody,' we said. And you said: 'Better bloody than empty'.

Galileo   Better bloody than empty. Pragmatic. Sounds like me. New science, new ethics.

Andrea   I of all people should have known. When I was eleven you sold someone else's telescope to the Venetian Senate. And I saw you put that instrument to immortal use. You would always laugh at heroes. 'People who suffer bore me' and 'In the face of obstacles, the shortest line between two points may be the crooked one'.

Galileo   I remember.

Andrea   In 1633, when it suited you to recant a popular part of your teachings, I should have understood: you were withdrawing from a pointless political squabble so that you could get on with the real business of science.

Galileo   Which is . . .

Andrea   The study of the properties of motion, mother of machines, which will make the Earth the only home we need and heaven can be abolished.

Galileo   Aha.

Andrea   You won the free time to write a work of science which only you could write. If you'd ended up at the stake in a halo of flames, the other side would have been the winners.

Galileo   They are the winners. And there is no work of science that only one man can write.

Andrea   So why did you recant?

Galileo   I recanted because I was afraid of physical pain.

Andrea   No!

Galileo   They showed me the instruments.

Andrea   So there was no plan?

Galileo   None.

Pause.

Andrea (*loudly*)   Science knows only one commandment:
serve science.

Galileo   Which I've done. Welcome to the gutter, brother in
science and cousin in treachery! O the irresistible glimpse of
a book, the holy commodity! The mouth waters and the
curses drown. What is the purpose of your work Andrea?
Surely the purpose of science is to ease human hardship.
The movements of the stars have become clearer: but the
people still don't understand the movements of their
masters. If scientists follow the orders of those in power, if
they store up knowledge for the sake of storing it up, then
science will be crippled and your new machines will bring
new forms of oppression. In time, you may discover
everything that there is to discover, you will progress but you
will progress away from humanity. The chasm between you
and them will become so vast that one day you will shout for
joy at some new achievement and you will be answered by a
world shrieking in horror. As a scientist I was presented with
a unique opportunity, astronomy had reached the market
square. One man standing strong could have shaken the
world. If I'd held out, scientists might have made a promise,
an oath, to use their knowledge solely for the good of
humanity! Now all we've got is a race of inventing pygmies
who can be sold to the highest bidder. I was never in any real
danger. For several years, I was as strong as those in power.
And I gave up my knowledge for them to use, or not to use,
or misuse, whatever suited them best.

Virginia *has entered with a dish and stands still.*

I have betrayed my vocation. A man who does what I have done cannot be counted amongst the scientists.

Virginia   You are counted amongst the faithful.

She comes forward and puts the dish on the table.

Galileo   That's right. I must eat now.

Andrea *holds out his hand,* **Galileo** *looks at the hand without taking it.*

Galileo   You're a teacher yourself now. Can you allow yourself to take a hand like mine? Someone passing through sent me geese. I still like to eat.

Andrea   Do you no longer believe that a new age has begun?

Galileo   Yes I do. Take care when you cross the border with the truth under your coat.

Andrea (*unable to leave*)   Regarding your opinion of the author of whom we were speaking, I'm unable to give you a reply. But I cannot believe that your devastating analysis will be the concluding word.

Galileo   Thank you very much.

He begins to eat.

Virginia (*showing* **Andrea** *out*)   We don't like visitors from the past. They agitate him.

Andrea *leaves.* **Virginia** *returns.*

Galileo   Who do you think sent the goose?

Virginia   Not Andrea.

Galileo   Perhaps not. How's the night?

Virginia (*at the window*)   Bright.

Fourteen

1637. **Galileo**'s book 'The Discorsi' crosses the Italian border.

And so across the border went
The book – and that's the end.
But we, hungry to know,
And him, are left at home.

Science's light if not used
For the good of all
May burn us in a rain of fire
And destroy us all
Yes all of us.

Small Italian frontier town early morning. Child playing at the barrier. **Andrea** *is waiting for his papers to be checked. He is sitting on a little chest reading* **Galileo**'s *manuscript.*

Guard   Why are you leaving Italy?

Andrea   I'm a scholar.

Guard   Under reason for leaving write scholar. I have to search your bags.

Boy (*to* **Andrea**)   Better not wait long. There's a witch lives here. She flies through the air at night.

Guard (*searching bags*)   What's this book?

Andrea   It's by the great philosopher Aristotle.

Guard (*suspiciously*)   And who's he?

Andrea   He's dead.

Guard (*to the* **Clerk**)   Have a look and see if there's anything about religion in there.

Clerk (*flicking through*)   I can't find anything. We can't examine everything. Then where would we be?

Guard   You can pass.

Luggage is collected by the coachman. **Andrea** *picks up the trunk and is about to go.*

Girl   There's that too see.

Guard   Stop!

Clerk   Wasn't it there before?

Girl   Devil put it there. I wouldn't touch it.

Guard   What's in that trunk?

Andrea   Books.

Guard (*to* **Clerk**)   Open it!

Guard   How many are there?

Andrea   Thirty-four.

Guard (*to* **Clerk**)   How long's that gonna take?

Girl   You're a scholar. Can people fly through the air?

Clerk (*who's begun an initial search through the trunk*)   All printed matter. Your breakfast's gonna go cold and when am I supposed to go over to the coachman and collect the outstanding toll money if I've got to go through all these books?

Guard   Right, we need that money. (*Gives the books a kick.*) Can't be much in there anyway. (*To coachman.*) On your way!

Andrea *goes with the coachman who is carrying the box over the border. On the other side, he puts* **Galileo**'s *manuscript in his travelling bag.*

Girl   Box has gone now. It was the devil.

Andrea (*turning round*)   No it was me. You should learn to use your eyes. Oh and I didn't answer your question. You can't fly through the air on a stick. Maybe if you had a machine on it. But we don't have a machine like that yet. Perhaps we never will because man is too heavy. But we don't know. There's so much that we don't know yet. We're really just at the beginning.

DRAMA ONLINE

A new way to study drama

From curriculum classics
to contemporary writing
Accompanied by
theory and practice

Discover. Read.
Study. Perform.

Find out more:
www.dramaonlinelibrary.com

BLOOMSBURY

methuen
drama

THE ARDEN
SHAKESPEARE

FABER
DIGITAL

9 781472 507419